JUMPSTART YOUR PUBLISHING DREAMS

Insider Secrets to SKYROCKET Your Success

What Others Say about *Jumpstart Your Publishing Dreams*:

"With equal parts inspiration and practical application, *Jumpstart Your Publishing Dreams* should be on every aspiring writer's shelf."
—**James Scott Bell**, best-selling novelist,
www.jamesscottbell.com

"Publishing is a complex business. Because Terry has been a magazine editor, an acquisitions book editor, and an author, he knows the inside scoop. *Jumpstart* captures his experience and serves it in easy-to-apply portions for every reader."
—**Michael S. Hyatt**, President & CEO, Thomas Nelson

"Terry's years of experience in traditional publishing makes him uniquely qualified to write this book. The 3rd paragraph on page 61 is worth one hundred times what you'll pay for his book and I recommend you buy two copies: Buy one for you, and one for an author you know whom you feel has lost hope in their ability to promote their book."
—**Alex Mandossian**, author, trainer and CEO/Founder of www.HeritageHousePublishing.com

"*Jumpstart* is the perfect title for this cornucopia filled with essential information that writers need more than ever to succeed. The resources that Terry includes alone are worth the price of the book. Terry's easy-to-read, generous advice comes out of his passion for helping writers and his decades of experience. *Jumpstart* will enable new or published writers to kick their career into high gear. I learned a lot from it."
—**Michael Larsen**, AAR, partner, Larsen-Pomada Literary Agents; author of *How to Write a Book Proposal* and *How to Get a Literary Agent* www.larsen-pomada.com

"Every writer should own and read this book, even those who are well established in their careers. This book can help writers achieve the goals for their writing and also help them see new possibilities they hadn't thought about before. I know I'll be taking another look at much of this advice"
—**Robin Lee Hatcher**, best-selling author of *When Love Blooms* and *A Vote of Confidence* www.robinleehatcher.com

"Insightful. Practical. Helpful. Energizing. Passionate. This book will move you closer to your dream of becoming a published writer."
—**Paul Mikos**, publishing executive,
www.publishingassociates.blogspot.com

"Terry Whalin has a real talent to explain to writers how they can customize their ideas for the best possible reception from editors and agents. *Jumpstart Your Publishing Dreams* has valuable insights into the publishing process."
—**Farley Chase**, Literary Agent, Chase Literary Agency

"Along the path to getting published, there are many possible sand traps for rejection which published writers have learned how to avoid. Follow Terry's expert and empathetic advice to take years off your learning curve."
—**Jacqueline Deval**, Publisher, Hearst Books and author of *Publicize Your Book* www.publicizeyourbook.com

"Terry's advice is practical, direct and easy to follow. You can't read a chapter of *Jumpstart* without feeling a little wiser. And that's not just for unpublished writers either."
—**Rick Hamlin**, Executive Editor, *Guideposts* magazine

"Here's the perfect primer for writers seeking to break into print or build lasting careers. Practical tips and encouragement abound, and the author's own career illustrates the soundness of his advice. A must-read for every aspiring author."
—**Joan Marlow Golan**, Executive Editor, Steeple Hill Books

"Terry understands what writers go through to get published. He has created a roadmap for any would-be writer to follow. You need the insight in these pages."
—**Rick Frishman**, Publisher, Morgan James Publishing, www.rickfrishman.com

"Terry Whalin's wealth of publishing experience combines with his practical teaching to give you the step-by-step insight that only comes from his years in this business. This book is perfect for anyone who has dreams and hopes of getting into print."
—**Raleigh R. Pinskey**, author of the best-selling *101 Ways to Promote Yourself*, www.promoteyourself.com

"*Jumpstart Your Publishing Dreams* stands out from the pack of 'how to succeed as a writer' advice—especially Chapter 11 on building a platform and chapter 18 on repurposing your content. These two chapters alone can double your publishing success this year."
—**Robert W. Bly**, Copywriter / Consultant, www.bly.com

"*Jumpstart Your Publishing Dreams* can offer you the ultimate pleasure of seeing your mission statement in motion, in the pages of your book, helping to make the world a better place."
—**Annie Jennings**, CEO Annie Jennings PR, National Media Specialists, www.anniejenningspr.com

"Terry Whalin's *Jumpstart Your Publishing Dreams*, manages to be both brutally realistic about the publishing world yet hopeful, almost spiritual, in its encouragement of writers. If this book doesn't get you motivated enough to finally publish your book, then nothing will."
—**Fern Reiss**, CEO of www.PublishingGame.com

"Terry has written the "go to" book for writers wanting to understand all the elements of today's publishing world. Few books are able to dispense this invaluable advice from someone whose experience is as diverse in the publishing world as Terry Whalin. Bravo, Terry."
—**Sharlene Martin**, Literary Agent, Martin Literary Management, www.martinliterarymanagement.com

"A smart, savvy guide every author needs—Terry Whalin's book brims with seasoned insider tips to getting published in today's ever-changing market."
—**Lisa Collier Cool**, past president of the American Society of Journalists and Authors

"I'm a big believer in telling stories. If you want to jumpstart your publishing dreams, learn how to tell stories. In this book, Terry shows you how to tell your own stories as well as how to capture the stories of others."
—**John Kremer**, author of the best-selling *1001 Ways to Market Your Books*, www.bookmarket.com

"Terry provides an excellent and comprehensive model for anyone to follow. His own publishing success, relationships with writers and editors, and years of teaching others are evident throughout the book. The process may be imperfect but a good guide is invaluable along the way. *Jumpstart Your Publishing Dreams* serves this role perfectly."
—**Dr. Brad Hamm**, professor, Dean of the Indiana University School of Journalism www.journalism.indiana.edu

"You need help from the rare person who not only has intimate knowledge of the process but can teach it to others. You will find that rare gift in Terry Whalin's book."
—**Sally E. Stuart**, author, Founder of *The Christian Writer's Market Guide* www.stuartmarket.com

"Terry Whalin is a godsend for aspiring writers as well as published authors wanting to stay afloat in today's market. In *Jumpstart Your Publishing Dreams* Terry becomes your own personal writing coach. These "insider secrets" will both help you define writing success for yourself—and then achieve it."
—**Kristi Holl**, Award-winning, middle grade (8-12) author, www.kristiholl.com

"Terry Whalin is an expert on publishing success. Aspiring writers would be wise to heed his advice closely."
—**Nick Harrison**, Senior Editor, Harvest House Publishers

"In addition to being a great writer and editor, Terry must be a magician. It's the only way he could put so much invaluable information in a single book."
—**Alton Gansky**, author of *Enoch* and 30 other books, www.altongansky.com

"Totally practical—actually DO his suggestions and you WILL become an author. Totally thorough—no stone is left unturned. This is an indispensable guidebook you will dip into again and again."
—**Diane Eble**, book publishing consultant, Words to Profit www.wordstoprofit.com

"Terry Whalin is the real deal! An experienced publishing pro respected by both sides of the aisle: authors and publishers. What's really going on inside this topsy-turvy business rarely resembles what you see on the outside. Terry's invaluable guidance will put you ahead of all the other 'wannabes' and within reach of your author dreams."
—**John Willig**, President & Literary Agent, Literary Services Inc. www.LiteraryServicesInc.com

JUMPSTART YOUR PUBLISHING DREAMS

Insider Secrets to SKYROCKET Your Success

W. TERRY WHALIN

NEW YORK

Published in New York, New York, by Morgan James Publishing. Morgan James and The Entrepreneurial Publisher are trademarks of Morgan James, LLC.
www.MorganJamesPublishing.com

The Morgan James Speakers Group can bring authors to your live event. For more information or to book an event visit The Morgan James Speakers Group at www.TheMorganJamesSpeakersGroup.com.

A FREE eBook edition is available
with the purchase of this print book

CLEARLY PRINT YOUR NAME IN THE BOX ABOVE

Instructions to claim your free eBook edition:
1. Download the BitLit app for Android or iOS
2. Write your name in UPPER CASE in the box
3. Use the BitLit app to submit a photo
4. Download your eBook to any device

ISBN # 9781630471095 PB
ISBN # 9781630471101 EB
ISBN # 9781630471125 HC
Library of Congress Control Number:
2008910806

All cartoons:
Copyright © CartoonResource.com.

Cover Design by:
Yvonne Parks (www.yvonneparks.com)

You can immediately download these two FREE Ebooks valued at over $84: *eBook Marketing Revealed, How to Write, Publish & Promote Your Own Profitable eBook!* and *Ghostwriters From the Inside Out.* Email info@wtwpress.com or register at our Web site: www.terrylinks.com/jump

Attention corporations, writing organizations, and writing conferences: Take 40 percent off and use this book as fundraisers, premiums, or gifts. Please contact the author:

W. Terry Whalin
9457 S University Blvd, Suite 621, Highlands Ranch, CO 80126-4976
(720) 708-4953 | terry@terrywhalin.com | www.terrywhalin.com

In an effort to support local communities, raise awareness and funds, Morgan James Publishing donates a percentage of all book sales for the life of each book to Habitat for Humanity Peninsula and Greater Williamsburg.

Get involved today, visit
www.MorganJamesBuilds.com.

Habitat
for Humanity®
Peninsula and
Greater Williamsburg
Building Partner

DEDICATION

First, I want to thank my wife, Christine, who has given amazing unconditional support throughout the creation of this book and beyond. Also I want to express my appreciation to Donna Goodrich for her careful editing and feedback. Many other friends and family have supported my work on this project. You know who you are. Thank you.

I dedicate this book to every writer and editor who built so much into my life and publishing experiences through telling your stories. While the names are too numerous to mention, I'm much richer for each experience. Thank you.

Finally I dedicate this book to every reader who carries dreams and aspirations to see their ideas appear in print. I hope these pages provide you with exactly what you need to jumpstart your publishing career. Seize the opportunity and go for it. I believe you can do it and that's why I've written this book.

TABLE OF CONTENTS

FOREWORD

During the 2007 Mega event in Los Angeles, I invited Terry Whalin to join our illustrious faculty. During this event as Terry and I talked for a few minutes, I saw his passion to help both new and experienced authors achieve their dreams of publishing.

Most people know me as the co-creator of the wildly-successful *Chicken Soup for the Soul* series which has sold an extraordinary 144 million copies worldwide. I understand what it's like to be a newcomer in the publishing world. Let me take you back to a time in my life more than 17 years ago when I faced the fears of everyone who wants to be published. When those fears showed up, I've learned that attitude opens doors. Always has. Always will. When you start on something, not everything will go smoothly. I believe if at first you don't succeed, so what?

When each of us begins to release whatever holds us back and we start to succeed, it makes everybody better off. As you are looking for this greatness in your life and focusing on your goal, be open to change. As you start down your pathway, be flexible and explore.

Have vision. Have a purpose that you are trying to achieve. Stick to it. You will find, I promise you, other people and other things, events, and opportunities will happen that you never imagined ahead of time. Be ready to change your course for success, because you may not know what it is right now. Do start with something because it will propel you forward.

In the early 1990s, Jack Canfield and I were encouraged to put our keynote addresses and workshops into a book. We discovered that translating what worked on the podium onto the written page proved more challenging than either he or I had anticipated. It was hard with our busy schedules to find time to get these stories on paper and editing them was an even bigger chore. After three long years, we had compiled only 68 stories—a far cry from the 101 we believed was the magic number for a successful book.

So we reached out to other professional speakers and asked them to submit their favorite stories for publication. The formula finally worked, and soon we were inundated with powerful tales of ordinary people doing extraordinary things. Previously we had too few stories; now we had too many. Once again, Jack and I turned to our friends and other professionals. We invited forty of them to read and rate each story on a scale of one to ten for its ability to clarify, move, and inspire. The 101 stories with the highest average scores were compiled into a final manuscript.

Our book still remained untitled. Many authors don't put much energy into their title because they believe the publisher will change it anyway. We knew the title of our book needed to be really good and committed to meditate on a winning title for *an hour each day*. Jack visualized the image of his grandmother's chicken soup and remembered how she told him it would cure anything. This book would have the same healing powers as that soup, but not for the body—for the soul. This concept birthed the book's best-selling title, *Chicken Soup for the Soul!*

After three long years, Jack and I were finally ready to approach publishers with our book. In the first month alone, thirty-three of New York's biggest publishing houses turned us down. For many authors, this wave of rejection would have been enough to make them quit. In the face of each rejection, we believed in our manuscript and instead said, "Next," then continued our search for a publisher.

These publishers told us, "Anthologies don't sell." Or, "We don't think there is a market for this book." Or, "We just don't get it." Or, "The book is too positive." Or, "It's not topical enough." A total of 140 publishers rejected our book. To top it off, our agent told us, "I can't sell this book—I'm giving it back to you guys."

In 1992, Jack and I attended the American Booksellers' Association Convention. We went from booth to booth talking to editors and sharing our vision of how our book would uplift humanity by helping people open their hearts, rekindle their spirits, and give them the courage to pursue their dreams. We left a copy of our manuscript with Peter Vegso, president of Health Communications, Inc. who caught the spirit of the book and soon agreed to publish it.

Our qualities of perseverance and determination with *Chicken Soup for the Soul* are some of the characteristics my friend Terry Whalin talks about in the pages of *Jumpstart Your Publishing Dreams.* Using Terry's insight and many years of experience in publishing, you can shorten the time it takes to locate your place in today's market. As you follow his practical advice, you will find ideas to create your own information business.

You and I are living in one of the greatest times in history. Take Terry's counsel to heart and apply it to your daily life. You will be able to go to places you never dreamed possible.

—Mark Victor Hansen

CHAPTER 1

Jump into the Water—the Imperfect Process

From my earliest memories, the printed page has played a key part of my life. Like many young parents, my mother read many books to me. When I was given a chance to select the book, Mom tells me I almost always chose *McElligot's Pool* by Dr. Seuss. Our family had most of this author's popular books. Many readers are probably saying, "*McElligot's Pool*"? Through the proliferation of *The Cat in the Hat, One Fish Two Fish Red Fish Blue Fish,* or the ever popular *Green Eggs and Ham,* many haven't heard of *McElligot's Pool.*

In the opening pages, a farmer laughs at the folly of a young boy named Marco who is actually called a "fool" because "You'll *never* catch fish In McElligot's Pool!" Then the farmer launches into all the reasons why the boy will not be able to catch any fish.

For the rest of the book, Marco spins an imaginative tale about what's really at the bottom of this pool and the wealth of possibilities connected to the sea loaded with fish. He concludes,

"Oh, the sea is so full of a number of fish,

If a fellow is patient, he might get his wish!

And that's why I think

That I'm not such a fool

When I sit here and fish

In McElligot's Pool!"[1]

From those early days, the dreams and spirit of imagination were stirred in my own life. They set me on a path to publishing which I continue walking down today. Over the years, I've fulfilled many roles within the publishing community: newspaper reporter, newspaper editor, magazine writer, magazine editor, editorial director, book author, book acquisitions editor, literary agent, publisher and online information marketer—someone who sells online information. The particular role is fluid and changes from day to day and sometimes I handle several different roles during a single 24-hour period.

How to Make the Best Use of This Book

Are you reading this book because you dream of being published and seeing your name in print? Or maybe you have been writing for a while and are looking for new opportunities to practice the craft of writing. One of the wonderful aspects of the writing world is that you don't have to be pigeonholed into a single discipline or area of the market. I know firsthand there are some advantages to specialization and developing an expertise in a particular niche. Yet at the same time, if you are receiving rejections in one area, you aren't stuck in that arena. With the fluid skill of a writer, you can easily adapt and move into another sector of the marketplace.

Through the pages of *Jumpstart Your Publishing Dreams*, I'm giving you a window into my own experiences in this market, combined with my practical how-to write information about the writing world. I recommend you read this book at least twice. In the first reading, look for new areas of the market that you can explore and practical tips you can immediately apply to your writing. Use a highlighter and mark those pages for additional study. Or use a series of Post-it® flags to mark different pages, and then during your second or third reading you can easily return to these pages.

Several years ago, my first how-to-write book, *Book Proposals That Sell*, appeared on the market. It's been gratifying and humbling to have people carry their copies of this book across the country to a conference where we meet face-to-face. They pull out these dog-eared and yellow highlighted copies and hand them to me so I can write a few words along with my name. Each time, I gratefully sign the book and return it to them. Yet inside, my mind asks the question, "Can I exchange this dog-eared book for a brand new copy? I'd even give them $20 for that much-worn book that I could take back to my office." Why?

Writing is a solitary experience. I sit at my computer and create words and stories. Inside I have the same insecurities as the next person, and that well-worn copy of my book which has served another person so well would provide me a constant reminder of the study and care that other people give these words.

This book is for you—the person who wants to be published or grow in your writing craft. Whenever I read a how-to-write book, I'm looking for one or two fresh ideas I can apply to my writing life.

If I find those ideas, then I consider the book a success because I've grown and profited from someone else's experiences. My desire is for your writing to thrive and move into a higher gear after you read these pages.

Repeatedly in this book, I point to the writing of others as I know my work stands on the shoulders of what I've learned from other writers. If you gain from these pages, please pay that gain forward through helping others.

The Value of Getting Published

On the surface, the path to publishing might not show you the diversity and range of possibilities for your writing. From speaking to hundreds of writers, I find many of them are focused on a particular area of writing such as writing a novel or a children's book. They haven't understood the value of learning good storytelling and communication skills that are relevant and useful for many different areas of writing. Because these writers are focused on a small niche area of publishing, it's almost like they are wearing blinders and can't see any other possibilities. In this section, I want to challenge you to remove your blinders and see the wealth of possible application for your writing within the publishing community. While each area of publishing has its own specific requirements, good writing and storytelling skills can be used in multiple areas to strengthen your overall career.

For example, you may want to write a book and have done a little exploration but the only companies who have responded to your questions are the publishers who want *you* to pay *them* to get your book into print. These companies are called self-publishers. Instead, you are looking for a traditional publisher who will pay you an advance, then print and distribute your book. Yet because you have no background in book publishing, you don't understand that 90 percent of nonfiction books are contracted from a book proposal and a few sample chapters, rather than a complete book manuscript. Without this critical detail, you have focused on writing a full-length book manuscript. Then you discover it may take you 12 months to find a literary agent who has to locate the right publisher. Then you learn it will take a longer-than-expected span of time for this publisher to release your book—normally 12 to 24 months *after* you turn in your manuscript. To a beginning writer, this realistic and practical publishing timeframe isn't evident on the surface.

Also, writers don't understand they can gain valuable training, experience, and exposure through writing magazine articles. From idea to assignment to publication with a printed magazine can be four to six months—a much shorter timeframe than books. Every editor is actively looking for writers who can communicate—whether they are a newsletter editor, an online editor, a magazine editor, a book editor or anyone else who has the title "editor." As a young magazine editor, I quickly learned I had to do less editorial work and could have greater confidence in assigning an article to a published author than an unpublished author. I read the ideas and considered giving the assignment to the unpublished author but their chances dramatically improved with any type of publishing experience.

Magazine and newspaper writers learn valuable skills that help their success with a longer project such as a book. These writers learn to write for a specific audience or publication and to write within a specific word length. Also through the writing process, they learn the value of a focused headline or title and relevant subheads scattered throughout the article, as well as hooking the reader with a tightly written opening. Then they continue to feed information to the reader as they structure their writing, and conclude the article with a focused point called a "takeaway." These writers also learn the importance of meeting a specific deadline (or a better way to stand out with the editor is to complete their assignment *before* the deadline). In addition, writers can learn the skill of rewriting and following an editor's direction. Sometimes your article will be "almost there" but not quite. Can you follow the editor's directions and complete the assignment to their satisfaction? It's much easier to learn about this process on a 1200-word magazine article than a 50,000-word book project.

Finally, these writers built trusted relationships with their editors—newspaper and magazine. Many of the editors I've worked with have moved up to higher paying publications or have become book editors or editorial directors. The seeds of my relationship with them were planted through my magazine writing. As a new writer you need to understand the necessity of building these lasting relationships.

"Moses, this chapter outline is really impressive."

Be Open to a World of Writing Possibilities

For a moment, let's explore a few of your options. Writing can take hundreds of different directions. The following is a partial list of some of the possibilities you may attempt. Each of us has different gifts and abilities. Your talents may shine in devotional writing while mine lie in nonfiction. One of the keys is to understand the broad range of possibilities and not to be focused on a single type of writing. For example, many people want to write books and simply ignore the magazine market which is far easier for the beginning writer and will reach more people than most books ever will. If you're stalled with your writing, consider a new direction. I'd encourage you to read the following list from time to time and see if you can open a new opportunity for your writing.

Advertising, Copywriting, and Public Relations

Advertising copywriting
Book jacket copywriting
Campaign development or product launch
Catalog copywriting
Direct-mail copywriting
Email ad copywriting
Event promotions/publicity
Fund-raising campaign brochure
Political campaigns, public relations
Press kits
Press/news release
Public relations for businesses
Public relations for government
Public relations for organizations or nonprofits
Public relations for schools or libraries
Speechwriting

Audiovisuals and Electronic Communications

Copyediting audiovisual
Business film scripts (training and information)
Educational/training film scripts
Corporate product film
Movie novelization
Radio editorials
Radio interviews
Radio commercials/public service announcements
Script synopsis for business
Screenwriting (original screenplays)
Script synopsis for agent or film producer
Scripts for nontheatrical films for education, business, industry
TV news story/feature
TV scripts
TV commercials/ Public Service Announcements

Book Publishing

Abstracting and abridging
Anthology editing
Book proposal consultation
Book proposal writing
Book query critique
Book query writing
Children's book writing
Content editing (scholarly)
Content editing (trade)
Copyediting
Fiction book writing
Ghostwriting, as told to
Ghostwriting, no credit

Indexing
Manuscript evaluation and critique
Nonfiction book writing
Nonfiction book collaborative
Novel synopsis
Proofreading
Translation
Work for hire

Business Writing

Annual reports
Writing for associations or organizations
Brochures, fliers, booklets for business
Business letters
Business plan
Catalogs for business
Corporate histories
Corporate periodicals
Ghostwriting for business (trade magazines or business columns)
Government writing
Grant proposal writing for nonprofits
Newsletters

Computer, Scientific, and Technical Writing

Computer-related manual writing
Email copywriting
Medical and science writing
Technical writing
Web page writing

Editorial/Design Packages

Greeting card ideas
Photo brochures
Educational and Literary Services
Educational consulting and designing courses for business or
    adult education
Educational grant and proposal writing
Writing for scholarly journals

Magazines and Trade Journals

Arts reviewing
Book reviews
Copyediting
Ghostwriting articles
Consumer magazine column
Consumer magazine feature articles
Trade journal column
Trade journal feature articles

Newspaper Writing

Arts reviewing
Book reviews
Column, local
Feature articles
Syndicated column, self-promoted

Miscellaneous Writing

Comedy writing for entertainers
Comic book or strip writing

Craft projects with instructions
Encyclopedia articles
Family histories
Gag writing for cartoonists
Institutional (school or church) history
Original prose story for comic book
Playwriting for the stage
Resumes

The Beginning of My Own Journey

Your journey to publication will be completely different from my experience. It will at times startle and surprise you. The writing business is a strange mixture of creative combined with practical "how-to" skills. These pages are signposts, and every step may not be critical for you. For example, you may not care about writing children's books or short stories, yet I would encourage you to read and explore that chapter. If you try it and it fits your writing style, it may be the key to expanding your writing world and I'd hate for you to miss it.

David Smith loved language and ignited an excitement in his English teaching at Peru High School in Peru, Indiana during the late 1960s. Of modest height with receding sandy hair and a bug-eyed appearance, Mr. Smith loved his students and reached out to challenge them. As the faculty supervisor for the school newspaper, Mr. Smith was always on the lookout for new talent to add to the staff. Thus he was excited when a gangly sophomore who had recently transferred from Towson, Maryland, caught Mr. Smith's attention with one of his written assignments.

One day after class, Mr. Smith pulled that teenager aside and said, "Terry, I think you would make a great addition to our newspaper writing staff. I'd like to invite you to our next staff meeting on Wednesday after school. Can you come?" At that point in the school year I had made few friends so I was flattered with his invitation. Another classmate, Jeff Reece, and I became the two sportswriters on the staff. Throughout the school year, I attended various sports events, collected sports data, and started interviewing people. Those first days on the staff newspaper introduced me to the writing world and the thrill of writing something for other people to read in print. Mr. Smith's simple invitation sent my life on a different career path and awakened my dreams of publishing. My writing became more than a dream; now it was rooted in practical experience and repeated opportunities to practice my craft.

The events in your experience will be distinct from mine, yet are equally important. There are vast opportunities in the publishing world for anyone willing to follow the steps to speed up their success. Welcome to an imperfect process. I'm excited about how the events will come together for your journey. In the next chapter, I will help you plan those first steps. When you are ready, turn the page and let's get started.

Two Sections to Help You Grow

Each chapter of *Jumpstart Your Publishing Dreams* includes two personal application sections. **Dig Deeper** provides a series of additional resources such as books and Internet sites, while **Awaken Your Dreams** asks a series of self-evaluation questions to help you make personal use of that chapter's material.

Dig Deeper

I created the Right-Writing.com Web site with the singular purpose of helping writers explore different types of writing. It contains thousands of pages of practical how-to information from different authors. Go to www.right-writing.com and explore each of the sections in the left-hand column. Plan to read a certain number of articles each day until you complete the entire site.

Also make sure you subscribe to the free newsletter as, by doing so, you will gain access to over 400 pages of additional how-to-write information available only to subscribers.

Awaken Your Dreams

1. Where are you in the writing journey? How would you categorize your writing experience? Beginner? Intermediate? Professional?

2. Jot down three goals for your writing, then take a moment and think about the size and scope of these goals. Are they big enough? The co-creator of *Chicken Soup for the Soul,* Mark Victor Hansen, encourages writers to set something that he calls Big Hairy Goals. On the surface, these goals may seem impossible but you want to stretch your imagination and possibilities. Create a Big Hairy Goal for your writing and put it on a note card you can carry with you in your wallet or purse, or put it someplace you will see it each day such as on your bathroom mirror. Each day focus on this Big Hairy Goal and how you can continually move forward to accomplish it.

CHAPTER 2

Plan, Then Work Your Plan

The word "instant" characterizes our world. Addicted to their email, many people have switched to a communication device which is much more than a cell phone but includes email so they are in constant touch with their work. These writers are committed to answering every single email that comes into their mailbox. I belong to several online groups and in one group, one writer answers every single question (whether she knows anything about it or not) and sends her response out to more than 700 writers. To me, it has become an annoyance and when I see her name in my box, I reach for the delete key and don't even bother to open it. Other writers worry if I don't respond to their emails within 24 hours.

How much time do you have during a single day to move toward accomplishing your publishing dreams? Are you planning and using your time wisely so you can move step-by-step toward the fulfillment of those dreams? There is an old saying in business: "If you fail to plan, you plan to fail." Or another version says, "If you fail to plan, you will be sure to hit it."

Consider These Time Wasters

Whether you have several hours a day or a full day to accomplish your writing goals, it is easy to fill those hours with "good things" that do not help you move toward the fulfillment of those goals. Let's examine some of the time wasters that can consume our time to write:

1. Email. It is easy to join various online groups and fill your email box with the communication from these groups. Without careful monitoring of your time, you can easily spend your day opening, reading, and answering these emails.

2. Regular mail. Do you receive a high volume of mail from various institutions? What about magazines, newsletters, and other publications?

3. Telephone calls. How much time do you spend on the phone chatting with friends and consuming the day with idle conversation?

4. Following the news. Until a few years ago, the release of world or national news came in cycles. Now we get a steady stream over our phone or computer or another media device. In the middle of such life noise, where do you find time to dream about publishing and succeed in those efforts?

5. Television. According to *USA Today*, the average person watches more than four hours of television *each day*. If you fall into this category, it is little wonder you are not accomplishing your publishing dreams. What are you willing to give up in order to reach your goals?

6. Family interruptions. If you have small children at home or a pet or an elderly parent, this could be a potential obstacle to your writing.

7. Volunteer obligations.

8. Writing opportunities. You may be surprised that I would include this aspect in the time waster category. When you begin to have your writing published, however, there are many "opportunities" for you, especially people who want you to write something without payment. Do these opportunities fall into helping you meet your long-term goals?

Have a Consistent Short-Term Goal

I've interviewed more than 150 best-selling authors about the elements of their success. They consistently state their commitment to a single goal and repeatedly focusing on this goal.

Several years ago, I had breakfast with Bill Myers, whose books and videos have sold more than eight million copies. I knew Bill was prolific so I asked for the secret of how he has accomplished the volume of writing year after year.

Bill held up his hand with his fingers spread apart and said, "Five."

I didn't understand so I asked, "Five what?"

"Five pages every day," he said. Even if Bill is attending a convention or a conference, he is committed to this goal of five pages a day—25 pages a week. "If I have time, I like to rewrite each page four times because I'm still learning my craft." This constant commitment to a short-term goal and meeting this goal day after day is one of the keys to accomplishing your writing goals.

Another person with a similar goal is novelist Bodie Thoene who has more than 45 million novels in print and won eight Gold Medallion Awards for her writing. Many people don't realize Bodie is severely dyslexic and does no pleasure reading, yet she writes page-turning novels. Like Bill Myers, Bodie also maintains a consistent goal of five pages a day. She sits at her computer hitting the keys with two fingers and may work until 10 p.m. to reach her goal—at least five finished pages. "No little elves come out of my closet to write 650 manuscript pages," Bodie said. "Some mornings I don't feel like writing, but I do it out of obedience to God. The opening scenes are always the hardest and can take as long as 10 or 20 pages," Bodie explains. With the opening pages behind her, the writing accelerates until she often completes 20 or more pages a day. Then her husband Brock reads the pages aloud to Bodie and they discuss any rough spots. "If I have to rewrite, I do it on the spot and never look at the pages again," she said.

Each of these writers accomplishes their short-term writing goal and then uses this benchmark to build and reach a larger long-term goal. It is a strategy you can also use to reach your publishing goals.

A Micro-Lesson about the Realities of Publishing

For over 20 years, I've been writing for publication, both magazines and books. During these years, I've written for over 50 different print magazines and I've also spent years as a magazine editor. My first book, a short children's book, was published in 1992 and since then I've written more than 60 books with traditional publishers such as Zondervan, Thomas Nelson, St. Martin's Press, Alpha Books, and Tyndale House Publishers. No one goes into a bookstore with the intention of finding a particular publisher, yet these name-brand publishers have a high standard in place that ensures the quality of their books. Traditional publishers know how to distribute their books through the best possible sales channels.

In addition to working with many different publishers as an author, for over five years, I worked on the inside of three publishers as a book acquisitions editor. I fielded submissions from individuals and literary agents and then championed the books internally at the publishing house, secured the publishing team's agreement about the value of a book, and negotiated the book contract. Because I've worked in almost every aspect of publishing, I have a unique perspective to write about the realities of the publishing business.

Whether I am participating in an online group or at a conference, I meet writers who have grown impatient with the publishing world and have decided to self-publish their work. If you have a book of poetry or short stories you would like to distribute to your family or friends, self-publishing is a good route. However, most writers don't think about distribution when they publish their book. When these writers self-publish their book, they take on the complete distribution, sales, and marketing for their product. It never crosses the uninitiated's minds how to sell the book. They assume that naturally their books will be sold through the local bookstore which is difficult to achieve. Self-publishing is, however, a viable alternative to authors who speak and can sell their books in the back of the room. You will need these types of outlets to sell books if you choose to self-publish.

Several years ago a pastor decided to self-publish a book of his sermons. Excited to have a printed book, he announced to an online group that he planned to spend a considerable amount of time the next few months contacting nearby bookstores and taking orders for his book. Unfortunately, this writer was operating under the false assumption that bookstores would carry his self-published book.

In fact, bookstores resist *any* self-published book and rarely stock them in their bookstore. The reason is that these books can't easily be ordered through the same system as traditional books and, in general, they don't sell. Because these books fall out of the normal procedures, they are often not returnable to the publisher. Unless you work inside publishing, you may have never heard that books can be returned to the publisher for the full price. Essentially they are sold to the bookstores on consignment and the stores have complex programs to monitor the sales of their titles. If the books don't sell within a typical time period of 60 to 90 days, they are returned to the publisher for a full refund. This practice presents a huge problem for traditional publishers who consider a good sale when a book has a 40 percent return or less. The self-published book falls outside of the normal channels for the retailer and with thousands of titles, he can't make a special effort for a single book.

To give you some additional understanding about book publishing, consider this statistic about iUniverse, one of the major self-publishing operations in the marketplace. According to a May 15, 2005 issue of *Publishers Weekly*, during 2004, iUniverse, a print on demand (POD) self-publisher, produced a total of 18,108 new books. Only *fourteen* iUniverse books were sold nationally through Barnes & Noble's bricks-and-mortar stores. While many people like to rave about their self-published books, where will they be able to sell them? This same *Publishers Weekly* article mentions that only 83 iUniverse titles (of the 18,108) sold at least 500 copies.

In May 2008, Bowker, the global leader of book production information, reported the 2007 U.S. book output was 411,422 books. While some of these numbers were self-published titles, traditional publishers released 276,649 new titles and editions. Because the typical bookstore carries about 10,000 to 15,000 titles, it is not surprising that you don't find your particular book in the store. When you understand this competition in the marketplace, it is still possible to get a book published but it's easier to start with a different and more achievable goal such as being published in a periodical.

While you may dream of getting a book published, this might be your long-term goal and you can plan some shorter goals for reaching this step.

Take Steps to Increase Productivity

Because I'm involved in publishing, publishers and authors will send me books to review. As an acquisitions editor, writers will send email pitches or book proposals or manuscripts in the mail for consideration. If I am not consciously organizing this material, it does not take long for the paper and books to overwhelm my work space and bottleneck any level of productivity. Maybe you've had this experience where the piles around you grow to such a level that you can't accomplish anything because you spend half of your time looking for a particular item. I've walked into the offices of some editors and they have paperwork piled everywhere. Some can barely reach their computer and desk because of the work piled around them. These editors have learned to work in the middle of such chaos but it doesn't work for me.

Another editor friend is so organized that she has each of the books on her shelf alphabetized by the author's last name. I'm definitely not that organized! The key to productivity for your publishing dreams is to create a system to tame the paper tigers in your life, the time wasters such as physical mail and email.

Let's return to the basic time wasters mentioned earlier and find a solution for each one.

First let's tackle your email. There is no rule that you have to read or respond to every single email. In fact, it is unrealistic to have this expectation. Also reevaluate your participation in online email groups with high volume participation. What value are you getting from this group? Can you drop out or go into a digest format and skim the responses? It is worth your examination to find a more effective way to handle these emails.

Veteran coach and management consultant David Allen has written a best-selling book I recommend called *Getting Things Done*. For every email or physical mail in your in-basket, Allen recommends you determine first, "Is it actionable?" If not, it goes into the trash, begins a tickler file so you can act on it later, or is filed for reference in a place you can retrieve it. If you look at the item and decide you can take action, then in less than two minutes, handle it (do it), delegate it (to someone else) or defer it (take action at a later date and set a specific time). These three steps move the items out of the holding pattern and into action or productive steps.

Combined with these steps, Allen recommends you process the top item first, then the other items one at a time, and you never put anything back into the "in" basket. Use these steps as you handle your regular mail as well as your email.

Next let's look at your telephone. When concentrating on a writing task, you don't have to reach for the phone when it rings. Let it go to voice mail. Alex Mandossian, the Internet marketing entrepreneur sets specific hours from 11 a.m. to 2 p.m. Monday, Wednesday, and Friday as his open call times for a new prospect or existing clients to phone him. There is no rule you have to be available 24 hours a day. Take control of your time on the telephone.

Another time waster is following the news continually throughout the day. Make a decision to limit this information and instead spend the time on your writing. It may take some concerted effort on your part to wean yourself from constantly monitoring an event but focus on the benefits and additional writing time you will gain from it.

How about the one-eyed monster or television as another time waster? As with the news situation, you may have to wean yourself from it but focus on the valuable writing time you will gain from such an effort.

Then there are family interruptions. Again, take control of this situation in your life. Hang a sign on the door or create a signal that you are occupied and unavailable unless something unusual occurs such as the building is burning. Make sure, however, you're available to family members at other times but not during the time you have set aside for your writing life.

Finally, let's tackle volunteer obligations and free writing opportunities. Do these obligations fit into your long- or short-term writing plans, or are they completely separate from your goals in this area? If the latter, then look for ways to disengage from these activities so you can focus on your writing goals.

Additional Productivity Secrets

It is a challenge for anyone to spend long periods of time at their computer writing. Perhaps it's easier for you to write in short bursts of energy and consistently spend 50 minutes of concentrated effort on your writing. After the completion of this stint, you stand up, stretch, and take a break, and then return to your chair to work another 50 minute session. It's been said that what your butt can't endure, your mind can't absorb. You will increase your productivity if you focus on shorter periods of time and write intensely during those shorter time periods. To focus on 50 minutes, use a countdown timer as a tool to put psychic pressure on you to get more done faster and better. You can get a free countdown timer at: www.timeleft.info and use it to increase your productivity.

Another valuable tool is to write down your plans for the next day before you leave your writing. Then throughout the night and before you return to your writing, you will have a definite plan about what you will write next. Some writers intentionally leave an incomplete sentence in their manuscript. This sentence allows them to return to the computer, open the file, and instantly begin typing on their document. Other writers will retype the last paragraph of their manuscript just to get their fingers moving.

In this chapter, I've only scratched the surface of productivity secrets. The key to jumpstart your publishing dreams is to organize and plan for the short-term and the long-term, then consistently move toward your goals and dreams.

Dig Deeper

1. You can gain more specifics about handling your email from Michael Hyatt's email tips at: www.terrylinks.com/Email1 and www.terrylinks.com/Email2

2. Download the countdown timer for your computer at www.timeleft.info and begin to use it each day.

3. Read the book, *Getting Things Done, The Art of Stress-Free Productivity* by David Allen, Penguin Books, 2001. This book is loaded with practical advice for everyone who wants to increase their productivity.

Awaken Your Dreams

1. Take some time to evaluate your own productivity with your writing life. Do you have a page goal for your writing? If not, can you create one that you can consistently execute?

2. Return to the various productivity suggestions in this chapter and choose which ones you need to apply to your personal life. Take action to increase your own productivity.

CHAPTER 3

Gain Publishing Experience

Within the world of publishing, there is a catch-22. Joseph Heller coined this popular term in his novel by the same name for a false dilemma where no real choice exists. In the first chapter, I alluded to this catch-22 when I mentioned something that I learned as a young magazine editor. With only a few experiences of assigning an article to an unpublished author, I determined the results would be more successful if I gave the assignment to an experienced published author. The reverse was also true. I discovered I had more work to do if I gave the writing task to an inexperienced and unpublished author.

Editors want to work with published authors, so for the unpublished the challenge is to get published in the first place and gain the experience. In the book area, as a publisher and former literary agent and acquisitions editor—I look for publishing credits as an indicator of the writer's knowledge about the business aspects of publishing.

When someone decides they want to be published, normally they mean that they want to get a book published. Millions of people every day dream about writing a book and selling it. According to Susan Driscoll and Diane Gedymin in *Get Published!* "…83 percent of Americans…say they want to write a book. Yet few ever do."[2]

If you propose a book idea to an editor or literary agent without any publishing experience, your idea is much less attractive than one from a published author. Why? Because each time someone is published in any format—not just a book—they gain valuable experience which can build for future publishing experiences. In this chapter, I want to show you how to overcome this objection from an editor and gain this required experience.

"As a famous writer, could you do something to help jumpstart my career?"

Knowledge Is Power

You are reading *Jumpstart Your Publishing Dreams* to gain knowledge and insight into the publishing business. I'm committed to giving tips and insight so you can use this knowledge for greater success with your publishing plans. Over the last 20 years in publishing, I've learned many lessons and I know for you to be able to absorb the information, I have to provide it in digestible chunks. My intention is for you to use these facts to overcome any possible barrier to your achievement and desire to be published. Without them, you will not be armed with the knowledge for your own success.

Many people falsely believe that when their book gets into print, it will naturally become a bestseller. It is possible to create a best-selling book and I'm going to provide you insights on how to foster this achievement. Every book is not a natural bestseller. In fact, the sales reality for books is startling to many people. "BookScan US provides a continuous market measurement of US retail book sales based upon electronic sales data analysis. Basically, we collect point-of-sale information from a variety of retailers and make this information available to the industry. In a typical week, sales of over 300,000 different titles are collected, coded and analyzed, producing complete market information for retailers, publishers and the media."[3] BookScan reported bookstore sales in 2004 from 4,000 U.S. retailers, excluding supermarkets, of the 1.24 million titles which are in print with these results:

10 titles sold . . . . . 1 million or more copies

22 titles sold . . . . . 500,000 - 999,999 copies

324 titles sold . . . . . 100,000 - 499,999 copies

767 titles sold . . . . . 50,000 - 99,999 copies

23,000 titles sold . . . . . 5,000 - 49,999 copies

67,000 titles sold . . . . . 1,000 - 4,999 copies

202,300 titles sold . . . . . 100 - 999 copies

948,000 titles sold . . . . . 1 - 99 copies

Average sale per ISBN through bookstores: 15 copies"[4] In other words, almost 80 percent of the books tracked sold less than 99 copies. And more than 95 percent sold less than 1,000 copies. When you read these statistics, you may wonder why anyone would want to write a book. Let me provide several additional bits of information. First, BookScan does not present the full picture of books which are sold in the U.S. For example, it does not track many of the smaller independent bookstores such as Christian retailers. Also, more than half of the overall sales numbers of books are sold outside of the bookstore in places such as book clubs and other outlets not tracked through BookScan. While the numbers are sobering, there are thousands of traditional publishers who continue to publish and sell books. With this sales history knowledge, you will gain a better understanding of why editors and literary agents make their decisions about your book idea submission. Be encouraged because there are possibilities out there but you need to be armed with the knowledge and power to catch these people's attention.

My Hard Knocks Submission Experience

As a young writer / journalist, I went to Indiana University which is one of the best journalism schools in the country. My journalism professors taught me a great deal about manuscript submissions. For example, my magazine writing class professor, Floyd Arpan, had a strict rule for the three ten-page magazine articles we wrote for his class. If he found two spelling or grammatical errors in our article, we received an automatic "F" on our assignment. This was in the days before computers and automatic spell check so I used a regular typewriter. If I made a mistake, I had to retype the entire page. It seems unnecessary to say that every submission should be without grammar or spelling errors—yet it happens a great deal. I often received submissions at my former literary agency in which the person misspelled my last name or even a word like "literary."

During my college class, I found Mr. Arpan's rule frightening. Thankfully, he had a redeeming factor of grace built into his rules. If we received an "F," we got a second chance to revise our work and turn it back in, and then he erased the first grade. When submitting the article the second time, we wrote a cover letter to a magazine and included a self-addressed stamped envelope. Mr. Arpan read the rewrite, recorded our grade, and mailed the submission. His effort eliminated a common barrier for many writers that prevent them from getting published. They write the material but never send their article out to an editor.

Years ago I was in a small writers critique group. One of our members was an unpublished novelist who had written seven or eight novels yet he'd never sent the material out for consideration. This writer got a lot of enjoyment from producing the material but had never learned how to market and submit his material. During the course of our critique time, we reviewed—and enjoyed—his novels and characters, and also encouraged him to send the material out for consideration. Today each of those novels has been published through traditional publishers.

As I think back on my magazine writing class in college, I was in the place of many beginning writers. I had zero understanding of the needs of the market or the editor or how to get my material into print. I learned many practical and life-changing lessons from this one class. For example, each publication has an intended audience. It is your responsibility as a writer to study the marketplace and be sensitive to meeting the expectations and needs of that audience.

In college I was clueless about how to meet those expectations. For example I wrote a story called "Gays and God" for which I interviewed a fundamental minister about homosexuality, and then a homosexual about his perspective about God and religion. Just to make sure I had a degree of balance in the story, I drove to Indianapolis and interviewed the lesbian pastor of a Metropolitan Community Church which is open to homosexuals. One of the main Christian evangelical magazines was *Christianity Today*. With zero sensitivity for the type of material they printed, I submitted my article to this publication. At that time *Christianity Today* didn't publish anyone unless they had a PhD or another higher level degree. In the years since, I've been published in this magazine but in this case, I simply received a pink form rejection of "Gays and God" in my SASE (self-addressed stamped envelope).

If you want to be published, you need to learn to think like an editor and be mindful of their audience. And to handle the catch-22 situation where I began this chapter—that you have to be published to get published—I encourage you (at least at first) to lower your expectations about where you want to be published. Instead of attempting a higher-paying magazine such as *Ladies Home Journal* or *Woman's Day* that requires a higher standard of writing, I encourage you to begin with a smaller magazine or newsletter. You may or may not be paid but you will have a greater chance of publication. The smaller publishing credits can build to something larger, but these credits can only build for you if you know where to start in the first place. As I've said, knowledge is power.

In general, the articles are short (between 500 and 1500 words) and as you write them, you will learn a great deal about publishing. These articles will teach you to write to a specific word limit. You will learn how to capture the reader's attention with a bang-up beginning. And as you work with the editor, you will learn something about the editorial process and other valuable lessons. Look for a magazine that publishes frequently as, obviously, a weekly magazine has a greater need for material than a monthly or a quarterly publication. If you want to be published, you are better off learning the ropes with a shorter piece than spending days and months on a book-length manuscript with the risk that it will never be published.

In this electronic age, I've learned my interaction with editors even via email is important. As my wife likes to remind me, you get only one chance to make a first impression. With an email message, it's almost too easy to fire off something that contains grammatical errors or spelling mistakes. It's important for every writer to think about such issues with their communication—and a reminder to myself as well. It makes me work harder at my email query letters or my nonfiction book proposals or any other type of writing. Your craft shows in every bit of communication. Often I will write something and set it aside for several hours, then return to it with fresh eyes. Or I will set it aside for several days and leave it as a "draft" in my in-box just to make sure I get all of the details correct.

Handwritten Submissions Still Exist

During my college years, our professors warned us that some writers submitted handwritten manuscripts and then they warned us about the folly of turning in material which was not typed. I listened to the caution but it seemed like an urban myth to me, something people proposed but didn't do. In summer school between my sophomore and junior years in high school, I learned to type and then consistently used that skill. When I studied journalism in college, in order to meet tight writing deadlines, I learned to compose my thoughts at the typewriter and pour them down on paper. I've used this skill every day for over 20 years. It never crossed my mind that someone would send in a handwritten manuscript—until it happened to me.

During the last seven years, I've reviewed and evaluated hundreds of book manuscripts. Working on the inside of a publishing house, you receive a lot of material and have to learn to deal with it quickly and efficiently or it will consume you. Decisions are made quickly and first impressions often become important. One day a writer called me and wanted to get together when she was coming to visit her family for a holiday in Glendale, Arizona. Before I agreed to meet with her I asked her what she had to discuss.

"I've written a novel," she confessed. As a former literary agent and now an acquisitions editor, I've been invited to numerous such meetings and I've learned to delay them until I have read some material from the writer. In a matter of minutes I can often tell if their novel is going to be something I want to publish, and there is little need to spend a lot of time in a meeting for that decision. I confirmed my mailing address and said good-bye and didn't think about it much more—until the package arrived which turned out to be my first handwritten submission. The package contained a full-length novel with over 100 handwritten pages in a bound notebook and with return postage. In some ways, I have to commend this writer for submitting her manuscript to me in the first place and I understand it was a great deal of work on her part to complete the novel. I read a chunk of her handwritten material, but there was little which was ready for a publisher. Before I spilled any coffee on it, lost any pages, or any number of other possibilities, I quickly wrote a rejection letter and returned it.

For insight on how editors and agents process and evaluate submissions, I suggest you read Noah Lukeman's how-to book, *First Five Pages: A Writer's Guide to Staying Out of the Rejection Pile*. To many people, it sounds cruel to think that after reading only five pages, anyone can make a decision. But as Lukeman writes, "Agents and editors don't read manuscripts to enjoy them; they read solely with the goal of getting through the pile, solely with an eye to *dismiss* a manuscript—and believe me, they'll look for any reason they can, down to the last letter."[5] Most editors and agents use a form rejection letter because they do not have time to craft an individual one. The publishing world is subjective. One person loves a manuscript and another rejects it. Your challenge as an author is to continually search for the connection to someone who will champion your work and get it published.

What You Gain with Publishing Experience

You will gain publishing experience in many different areas if you lower your expectations. Instead of a singular focus on writing a book, I'd encourage you to look for opportunities to get your work into print. Yes, you can also write online on such places as Web sites or newsletters but writing which appears in a printed form often has a higher standard and is more valued among the editors.

The publishing marketplace is diverse and no single individual has all of the answers or insight. Yet I've read a terrific resource, *You Can Write!* by Sheryl Fullerton & Naomi Lucks. Several years ago I met Sheryl, executive editor at Jossey-Bass, at a writer's conference. *You Can Write!* is loaded with sound wisdom and I want to give a small example. In chapter 13, Fullerton and Lucks give the "Nuts and Bolts of Book Proposal Format and Style." A subsection called "Take a Good Last Look" suggests hiring a professional editor before you send out your proposal and sample chapters. They say, "If you can't afford to or don't want to hire a professional editor, go over the whole thing very carefully yourself. Ask a couple of intelligent friends to do the same and invite their candid comments (and sharp-eyed proofreading skills). Here are a few things to watch out for:

- Look for obvious mistakes—we all make them. Missing words, typos, and other common errors are easy to miss when you're familiar with your proposal.

- Use your computer's spell-checker, but don't count on it. It doesn't know if you meant "there," "they're," or "their," but you do."[6]

They include three additional valuable suggestions, but you get the point. This book is loaded with insight and the voice of experience. It is well worth your time to read and study it.

Plan to Start Somewhere

Too often would-be writers look at best-selling authors and think they seem impossible to imitate. From my publishing experience, I know it's a long shot and takes hard work to create a bestseller. Yet at the same time, I understand that each author started in the same unpublished state that you may be in right now. Can we learn something from the early steps of these authors?

Biographies are a wonderful place to discover some of these early experiences such as in the biography of Dr. James Dobson called *Family Man* by Dale Buss, a former reporter for the *Wall Street Journal*. The writer presents a carefully researched and documented—yet realistic—picture of Dr. Dobson, who includes best-selling author among his many accomplishments. Here's a paragraph from this book which illustrates some of Dr. Dobson's early beginnings in publishing. It relates to his first book, *Dare to Discipline*, which has sold millions of copies and was released in 1970.

> Zondervan and Tyndale House each offered Dobson a contract, the latter padded with an advance of five thousand dollars. Word didn't enter the derby, Dobson recalls, because the company already published the books of another family-advice expert named Charlie Shedd. Dobson couldn't decide which publisher to favor, but Heatherly [Doc Heatherly who had just retired as the director of marketing for Zondervan] recommended Tyndale House because of the marketing expertise of an executive named Bob Hawkins [who a few years later began another publishing house called Harvest House Publishers]. That was the tiebreaker for Dobson. A mere six months later, after a feverish writing effort, *Dare to Discipline* was published by Tyndale House. Dobson requested 250 copies of his freshly printed treatise to send to friends and colleagues. He autographed them all, then he and Shirley carefully packaged each one of them, addressed the envelopes, stamped them, and wrote fourth-class instructions on the labels. Then they knelt beside the pile of books and laid their hands on the packages as they prayed. They dedicated the work to the cause of Christ, loaded them into the back of their red Volkswagen Beetle, and took them to the post office. It was the last time Dobson would have to do that sort of thing himself.[7]

Tyndale House has published the majority of Dr. Dobson's books over the years.

I personally found these initial steps fascinating reading. If you haven't published anything, where will you begin the process? It is different for everyone. Many writers hone their craft in the magazine area before they write their first book. Others write a proposal and enter the publishing world in the book area. The key is to be actively involved in the process at some entry point. Don't stand on the sidelines but jump into the water and begin this process of building a body of work. I didn't suddenly wake up and write for more than 50 magazines and publish over 60 books. The process happened gradually over time. It can be the same for you.

Dig Deeper

1. On his Web site at http://www.lukeman.com/greatquery/Noah Lukeman gives a free copy of an Ebook called *How To Write A Great Query Letter*. While Lukeman is writing about book queries, much of the information is also relevant for magazine writing or any type of publication.

2. Get a copy of *The First Five Pages: A Writer's Guide to Staying Out of the Rejection Pile* by Noah Lukeman http://amzn.ro/19DHRjG

3. Explore Sheryl Fullerton and Naomi Lucks' Web site: http://www.youcanwrite.com/ and also get a copy of their excellent book, *You Can Write It* at http://amzn.to/1gszA1o

Awaken Your Dreams

1. Take time to target several magazines in which you want to be published.

2. Write several query letters each week to these publications and target them until you reach them. It will take persistence and continued effort to reach your goals.

CHAPTER 4

The Value of Apprenticeship

I loved to hear Jack talk about his work but I did not understand his passion for the craft of ironworking. Each day in the Dallas, Texas summer heat or the bitter cold of winter, Jack enjoyed dangerously hanging off twenty-story buildings to weld two huge pieces of iron into those buildings.

To learn his craft Jack took classes at night but also worked as an apprentice in the shadow of a journeyman ironworker. Eventually he earned the right to become a journeyman and train another apprentice. This type of skill and training is common in crafts such as plumbing, masonry, and ironworking. When it comes to the craft of writing, however, few people value apprenticeship. Instead many writers have the mistaken idea they can instantly sit over their computer keyboard and pound out the next best-selling nonfiction or novel without training.

In this chapter I want to give some ideas about how to apprentice as you gain key knowledge to advance your skill as a writer and jumpstart your publishing dreams. Some people find a writing coach or mentor to help them in this process. The bulk of my apprenticeship as a writer has been informally learning from someone else or reading their how-to write book instead of a formal mentor relationship. A critique group is a much more typical and helpful way. This chapter will provide detailed information about forming and participating in a critique group that can help you advance your skills as a writer.

Cautions About An Editor's Feedback

Through my teaching at writer's conferences, I meet many writers pitching their ideas. When I was a magazine editor, these writers pitched article ideas. When I was an agent, they came with nonfiction and fiction book ideas. Now as an acquisitions editor, they continue to meet with me about their dreams of appearing in print.

Typically, during a conference, faculty members meet with individual writers for 15 to 20 minutes during which they listen to their ideas and give a few sentences of instant feedback. I take this responsibility seriously and when I talk with these writers, I always try to couch my advice with some cautions. I recall the early days of my writing life when I hung onto every word from these editors. As a new writer, I forgot about one of the key issues with the editor's feedback—that the editor is not perfect but can make mistakes with their advice. I often took detailed notes as the editor spoke so I could revise my work and meet their expectations.

At one conference, I showed my book proposal to an editorial director. As I sat patiently, he looked through my work and gave instant feedback while I furiously captured his insights on a legal pad. This professional worked for a house that had published one of my books and now I had a 30-minute appointment. What a great relational building time for me. I returned home armed with my notes and promptly tackled the revision. Because I had a full-time job, my writing was squeezed into spare evenings and weekends. It took a few weeks for me to complete this revision, and then resubmit it to this editor. I waited a number of additional weeks before I received his response. With great expectation I opened the envelope—only to receive a form rejection.

This editorial director didn't recall our conversation or his instructions for revision. Through this hard lesson, I learned to take this type of feedback with a grain of salt. Until there is a publishing contract or a firm obligation to publish your work, any such feedback is speculative. Years later, I have a greater understanding about what happened from that editor's perspective. The back-to-back meetings with authors at these conferences are grueling and wearing for the editors. The specific words of advice—no matter how experienced— are difficult to monitor and much less recall.

As an acquisitions editor or former literary agent, I meet with many writers. One blonde-haired mom proudly presented a large bound notebook containing her novel manuscript. As I held it in my hands, I gushed, "Congratulations for completing your novel. What a great accomplishment."

"Thank you. Each evening after I put my small children to bed, I wrote for 20 minutes a day over a four-year period," she said. I admired her tenacity to complete the book. Yet when I looked at the text, in a glance I could see the story needed lots of work to be ready to publish. At the end of the session, I returned it to her. Through hard experience and years of observation, I've seen that it often involves completing the third or fourth novel before an unpublished novelist finds their storytelling stride and gets published. Many of those first attempts—even from much published novelists—are still hidden in desk drawers away from the public.

Whether I am on the faculty of a writer's conference or reading my physical mail or my email, I review a high volume of submissions. Many times I compare it to panning for gold. I have to sort through many stones before I find something worthy of detailed attention. Unlike some authors I've met, I don't have a photographic memory. I can't remember every one of these manuscripts that I've reviewed. Occasionally I will attend the same conference two years in a row. One year a gray-haired distinguished woman talked with me about a proposal for a devotional book. At the encouragement of her local church, she had written a number of her personal experiences into short one-page readings combined with a simple prayer and a Bible verse. In today's market, it is a challenge for an unknown writer to get books of this category into print. The writing may be excellent but a lack of an insider understanding about how these types of books are published is one of the hurdles to publication. In the few minutes we had to meet, I carefully explained to this writer about book packagers or the middleman between the writer and the publisher. On a contract basis from the publisher, these book packagers locate the designer and writer and then produce a book ready to go to the printer. They relieve the day-to-day pressure on a publisher's in-house editorial and design employees, yet allow the company to produce more books in a shorter time frame.

I referred this particular writer to several different Web sites for additional explanation, talking fast because of the compressed time for our meeting. As I talked, she took notes, nodded her head, and appeared to understand the explanation. Those words marked my last interaction with this writer—until about 12 months later at the same conference. As I looked over her material, it "seemed" familiar to me. When I asked a few questions, I received a string of excuses, combined with the admission that she was showing around the same project as the last conference.

My experience with this woman is actually a common experience with writers who are stuck and have no idea how to expand their idea. In the pages of this book, I want to give you some tools to take action on your dreams and desires for your writing.

How Do I Get Published?

This question always seems to catch me off guard, but it should not surprise me. It's a frequent question on my Right-Writing.com Web site.

In high school and college, we are required to write papers. Many people believe they can turn their love of storytelling into print. Unfortunately, they are lost as to where to begin the journey. Many of them decide to write a children's book. Others opt to write a novel. Yet another group begins a nonfiction manuscript. Because they have persisted enough to begin, they figure someone should publish the material. They've done nothing to think about the market for their particular writing or who will publish it. This is a key mistake on their part. Before you write one word, you need to focus on your reader. Who will be interested and how can you write your material so the editor for those readers will accept it?

Often these individuals believe they can write their novel and the first editor who reads it will love it and publish it. Then they will be on the best-seller list. This common belief should not surprise you. We live in an instantaneous world. If we don't reach someone on their phone, we call their cell phone number. Something must be wrong if we don't get a 24-hour response to an email. But writers need to realize the publishing world doesn't move fast and often it takes a while to receive a response—particularly a "yes" response.

It's the road few travel but I strongly believe in the principle of apprenticeship. Instead of planning on writing the next bestseller, you learn to be an excellent storyteller. You practice your craft with magazine or newspaper articles. Instead of writing an untargeted novel, you learn to craft a short story with a page-turning plot and realistic dialogue and characters.

Instead of planning on writing the next nonfiction bestseller, you learn to write different types of magazine articles for a small publication. Rather than being concerned about the royalty rate or the amount of payment for the article, you celebrate whenever anything appears in print where others can read and appreciate it. Often beginning writers get hung up on things like royalties and rights instead of focusing on quality work.

To me, the journey isn't a onetime experience. It's a matter of building a body of work—solid writing over a long period of time. As you get published in one publication, the experience gives you the opportunity to be published in another market. You learn how to meet the editor's needs and, as a result, the reader's needs.

I've read stories of people who catapult onto the best-seller list with their first novel. It has happened and will happen in the future; however, it's simply not the normal experience in publishing. I encourage writers to learn their craft, work hard at their storytelling, and eventually they will be published—and not just once but many times and consistently. It's a journey worth the trip and one filled with learning every step of the way.

Writers Are Insecure

I'll admit it. Writers are an insecure bunch of folks—and I'm one of the first to stick up my hand and confess this quality. As creative types, we pour ourselves into our work. If it's a novel, we get totally wrapped up with our characters and the dialogue and our plot twists and turns. If it's nonfiction, we are providing how-to information to drive the reader in a certain direction. If it's a magazine article, it has a particular slant and point to it.

When we tuck our manuscript or book proposal into an envelope and send it into the market or write a query letter to an editor, we are putting ourselves out there. It hurts to get rejected and turned down. I know it's just business and not personal, but we still believed we were sending our manuscript to just the perfect place—and the answer back to us was no. It's unfortunate, but some writers get so bothered with the responses, they never submit their materials to be published.

My experience as an editor and agent has shown me that novels are often submitted prematurely. The writer hasn't learned the craft of writing or skill of storytelling. Many of these novels are simply clogging the publishing world. In one sense, you admire the courage of these writers to get it out there—but because they usually receive only form letter rejections, they have no idea how to fix their work. The editors can't give you this feedback. You learn to grow in your craft through the critique process. As writers, we need to become tough skinned and continue to get our material out into the marketplace—and work to find a home for it.

The Necessity of Persistence

How persistent are you in getting published? This business ebbs and flows. Some days you feel like you are on top of the world and other times it seems like all you are garnering is rejection slips. The mood can vary from day to day (or even hour to hour).

For more than 20 years, I've been involved in writing and publishing. It varies for me as well. Yet I persist because I'm devoted to this business—even if it is difficult. The key is to keep working at it.

To gain some insight for this topic, I turned to one of my favorite how-to-write books mentioned earlier—*The First Five Pages, A Writer's Guide to Staying Out of the Rejection Pile*. Whether you have been multi-published, never published, or someplace in between, I recommend a thorough (and even repeat) reading of this book. The author Noah Lukeman is a New York literary agent. He has learned a great deal from his experience which he builds into this book. In the Epilogue, he writes,

> Getting published is hard these days, even for great writers, even for writers who have been published before. With the conglomeration of major publishers and the fear of the "midlist" book, many fine books will never make it into print.

> Do not be discouraged. If you stay with it long and hard enough, you will inevitably get better at your craft, learn more about the publishing business, get published in a small literary magazine—eventually find an agent. Maybe your first book won't sell; maybe your second or third won't ether. But if you can stand the rejection, if you can stubbornly stay with it year after year, you *will* make it into print. I know many writers who wrote several books—some over the course of thirty years—before they finally got their first book deal.

> You must ask yourself how devoted you are to getting published. Yes, a lot of the publishing process is out of your control. You might, for instance, have just missed your big deal at a publishing house because a book similar to yours was bought the week before; or you might get a green light

from every editor in the house and then get turned down at the last second because the editor in chief or publisher—or even a sales rep—personally didn't like your book. But a lot of the process—a lot more than you think—is in your control, and this is where devotion comes into play...The ultimate message of this book, though, is not that you should strive for publication, but that you should become devoted to the craft of writing, for its own sake.[8]

Acquire Thick Skin

For more than 20 years, a college assignment from my first journalism class has been tucked into a folder. Occasionally I pull it out and look at it. Why keep it?

Each page of the paper is filled with red ink from my college professor. After pages of marks for improvement and changes, I found this final comment, "Terry, you do a very commendable job of assessing Greeley's [Horace Greeley, the journalist from American history] and Hearst's [William Randolph Hearst] impact on journalism, but say nothing about their effect on society. B"

My grade and the comment deflected a bit of the impact of the red ink. It's an example of how journalists need to develop a thick skin. Every writer needs to receive and process feedback about their writing. They find a topic and write about it to the best of their ability. The editor takes that writing and improves it, then returns it to the writer for their input. How will you handle the review portion of the process? Admittedly it's not for the fainthearted. And what's the value of my old journalism assignment? It's a constant reminder to me that I need to keep learning as a writer. I need the input of my editor and others in the publishing process. It's only as we focus on excellence that excellence results. I need to develop a thick skin so I can receive and fairly process this type of information. A great deal of my development in this area happened over 20 years ago. It's a solid reminder to each of us with our writing.

Two of my recent books used the "reviewing" feature of Microsoft Word. If you aren't familiar with this editing feature, it is not for the thin-skinned writer. The deadlines for these books were fairly short in terms of the time to write the manuscript. I delivered the writing in portions or stages to the editor. After I wrote the first portion, and while I was writing to the second deadline, my manuscript went through four or five different editors. Each editor used a different color pen for their comments. These comments and edits and questions were inserted directly into my manuscript.

Weeks later when I received my manuscript, it was a rainbow of colors and not just in a few places of the manuscript. Almost every sentence included a variety of comments and potential changes. My responsibility as the "author" was to answer any questions and fix any issues raised—again in a short amount of time—and still maintain a professional attitude rather than take it personally.

Get Your Writing Moving—Join a Critique Group

Discouraged about your writing? Wonder if you are ever going to get anything published? How do you learn to write? Admittedly, any kind of writing requires work and effort, but joining a critique group can move you in the right direction.

A critique group is a small group of writers who encourage each other and provide regular help. Joining a group is not something to be taken lightly. It means a commitment to write something each week or month, polish the writing, and then share it with the group. Also it's a commitment to carefully critique the other members' manuscripts.

"Sounds wonderful," you think. "Where do I find one?"

First, see if your local writers group offers critiquing. If you write children's material, the Society of Children's Book Writers and Illustrators has critique groups scattered across the country. Determine your area of specialization such as fiction, children's writing, articles, scripts, poetry, and if there is not a group in your specialty or area, why not begin one?

"Oh, no," you wail. "I'm a beginning writer. I need someone to teach *me*."

Each of us begins somewhere if you are willing and available. You can learn lots through a critique group. You simply set the time and place, then announce it in your local newspaper or radio/TV community calendar. Be creative in your networking and be available to begin a group and minister to others who want to write.

You need to determine where you will meet and what time. Decide on the maximum number of participants and how often the group will meet. The larger the group, the more time will be needed for each person's manuscript. A small number is often better.

Once you've located the people, how do you begin? One essential requirement is that people be committed to writing as well as willing to critique other writers' materials. If people do not bring materials, the group degenerates into a social time rather than a work session.

Regarding the actual critique, there are three options. Some groups bring manuscripts to the meeting, read them aloud, and then critique them. Others mail manuscripts ahead of time and then talk about the content during the meeting. (I prefer the latter method since I find it difficult to catch the content from reading aloud. In my opinion, the manuscript receives a better critique when read in advance.) Another option is to bring enough copies for everyone and have silent critiques, giving the manuscripts back to the writer at the end of the meeting with written comments.

During the meeting, agree on the amount of time for each manuscript so no one person or manuscript dominates the critique session. For example, a group of four may meet for one hour each month and spend 15 minutes on each manuscript.

Now you have someone else's work. What do you do with it? First, begin with praise. Find something that you like about the manuscript—the format, main character, or the general theme or plot. In this way, we build up one another and give encouragement.

Critiques vary according to the type of material. Here are some basic questions to consider for nonfiction, then fiction.

How to Critique Nonfiction:

1. Examine the overall structure. Is it logical? What kind of article is it and does it fulfill the proper requirements? Can you state the premise in a single sentence? Does the article clearly point out the problem, and then offer a sensible conclusion? Is there adequate information for the reader to draw his own conclusions and learn what he needs to learn? Is it easy to read? Entertaining? Does the writing show rather than tell? Are there illustrations and anecdotes and are they effective?

2. Detailed examination. Are the facts accurate? References correct? Transitions smooth? Point out any awkward phrases, incorrect grammar, misspellings, and trite phrases. Is the title eye-catching and appropriate? Do you want to keep reading after the first paragraph?

How to Critique Fiction:

1. Overall examination. Did you like the story? Why or why not? Did it work as a whole? Who was the main character? Did the beginning set up an immediate, important (to the character) problem? Was the fictional dream maintained? Were there rough spots? Was the main character's behavior consistent? The other characters consistent? Did the story have a beginning, middle, and end? If in a particular genre, did it work? Is it appropriate for the chosen audience? Were the plot and the character's motive in sync? Was the tone appropriate? The pacing? What was the theme? Did it work? Can you state it in a single sentence?

2. Detailed examination. Did the author tell rather than show the story? Point out any awkward phrases, incorrect grammar, misspellings, trite phrases, and poor transitions. Were there any metaphors or analogies? Did they work? Was the dialogue realistic? Did it forward the plot? Did the first paragraph grab your attention? How about the title? Was there a balance of narrative and action? Was the sentence pattern varied?

These questions, whether for nonfiction or fiction, reveal the critiquer's commitment. It's a lot of work to carefully examine another person's work.

The Advantages of a Critique Group

Finally let's examine some of the advantages of being in a critique group. First, it provides you a writing deadline. Each week or month the group needs to keep writing and that means constantly producing new material. This deadline will push you to schedule time for writing and polishing your work.

When other writers examine your manuscript and critique it, the process gives you an edge over other freelancers. Other writers can give you fresh insight, marketing ideas, and help on the manuscript before an editor sees it. This extra polish makes your manuscript stand out from the others on the editor's desk.

The critique group provides an excellent atmosphere to exchange ideas with other writers. You get the benefit of receiving their input, experience, and encouragement. Showing your manuscript to another person involves risk, however. What if they don't like it? Better to hear that from a fellow writer and polish it some more, than send the article all over the country, receive rejection slips, and never know why. Take the plunge and either begin a group or join an existing one.

After a critique session, I collect the input from my group. I don't always take their comments but I follow most of them. I add these corrections into my article and polish it before sending it out to the editor. The process works for me and has helped give my writing an edge over others who don't take advantage of help from other writers. It will help you avoid those form rejections and get some publishing credits.

The Horror of Typos

While I continually work at my writing, I am not perfect and I wanted to show you in this example that I make mistakes yet still grow from them:

When someone calls to your attention a typographical error in a printed document, how do you respond? Do you shrug it off as someone else's responsibility or leap into action? And what if an even worse situation happens—the person points out the typos in a very public forum—yet doesn't bother to send the information directly to you? It may sound farfetched but it does happen as you will see in this true story. One of the truths that I've learned about publishing and writing is that the devil *is* in the details.

During a rare moment, I look at customer reviews of some of my current books listed on Amazon. I have the active books organized in my Amazon profile so it's pretty simple to check them. I have participated in a program called an Amazon Short and my article is called *Straight Talk from the Editor, 18 Keys to a Rejection-Proof Submission.* For the first six months of their contract, Amazon had an exclusive on this project but then it switched to a non-exclusive relationship. It continues to sell on Amazon, yet you can get the same material free in the Dig Deeper section of this chapter. Because I have the source document for my version, I can easily update it and keep it current. Also the links inside this version are "clickable," something that Amazon doesn't allow with their Amazon Shorts. While the text is the same, the format and appearance is different to make the two products distinct.

Imagine my horror when I read the four star review from Desert Gal dated February 17, 2008, with the headline, "Good Tips...Poor Spelling." I appreciated the kind words, and then I read the details of the second paragraph. When I opened my version and searched for the specifics from Desert Gal, yes, I located these misspelled words in the Amazon Short. It has been well over a year since I've read this material. I put it through several checks—and Amazon has an editor who reviewed it and then mostly worked to format the document. The homophone (tender versus tinder) was completely missed. I corrected these errors and they are not present in my version.

If I had not read the reviews, these errors would still be present. Instead of copying me or contacting me directly, this former editor chose to write her review on Amazon which is not the best way to reach me. If you find a typo in a book or published document, it is much better (and direct) to contact the author or the publisher and get it resolved, instead of airing it in a public forum and then hoping the author will read it.

Recently I was looking at a new book online which was offering 101 bonus gifts. One of the gifts from an author named Tim had his name spelled "Time." I pulled up my Snag-It program, copied the screen, and sent a note directly to this author. He is now informed and can go through whatever steps to fix this matter.

Despite the best efforts and check systems from publishers, mistakes do creep into printed materials. The good news is that they can often be fixed. Last year in my daily Bible reading, I found a small section which made no sense. I pulled up my Bible program and discovered about 50 percent of a verse was missing in this printed book. I took a few minutes to contact my friend, the editorial director of this publishing house. He wrote back and expressed appreciation. A week or so later to my complete surprise, the publisher sent a leather-bound version of this Bible with a handwritten note of thanks. With that type of appreciative response, if I find something else in this book, I'm inclined to pass the information on to them. From my experience, the direct approach to the author or publisher is often the best approach for resolution.

Throughout this chapter, I've been encouraging you to use a variety of resources to learn about the craft of writing and keep growing in this craft. It's a process which will never end, but will take you to a higher and higher level of visibility in the writing world.

Dig Deeper

1. To learn more about forming a writing group or developing a one-on-one mentor relationship, there are a couple of resources which I recommend. First, *Writing Alone, Writing Together: A Guide for Writers and Writing Groups* by Judy Reeves (New World Library, 2002). This book covers the nuts and bolts guidelines for forming and running groups of various kinds, along with savvy strategies for navigating the emotional ups and downs of groups, plus it includes information about conferences and retreats, colonies, associations, and open readings.

2. The second book I recommend is *The Writing Group Book: Creating and Sustaining a Successful Writing Group* edited by Lisa Rosenthal (Chicago Review Press, 2003). If you have decided to write for a living, brace yourself. You probably already know this life is at times lonely and often filled with rejection. One of the easiest ways to overcome these feelings is to gather sympathetic writers around you and have a regular time to meet. As Lisa Rosenthal writes in the introduction to this excellent resource, "The first step is regularity. Meeting at a specific time and place creates deadlines and a community that members can count on, and as familiarity with each other's voice grows, the helpfulness of feedback increases, and members become more invested in each other's work."

Rosenthal has pulled together an amazing collection of essays from different types of writers and different writing situations. The book is organized into four sections. The first portion focuses on the basics such as starting a writing group—whether face-to- face or online—and with writers of different genres and experience levels. The second section emphasizes constructive critique and also teaches how to maintain a fruitful writing group in spite of conflicts and various other challenges. The third section provides various insights into why some groups flourish and other groups fizzle, and loads of advice on how to keep your group moving ahead. The final section gives different ideas on how to move the writing group to a broader level of visibility through publishing anthologies and sponsoring group events. The back of this book features some simple tips for specific groups such as playwriting, and how to market your work.

Awaken Your Dreams

1. In the writing community, you do not need to work in isolation. You can be connected to a mentor and a critique group, but it will take some initiative and effort on your part. Take time in the week ahead to explore the local possibilities. Is there an existing group that you can join and meet with on a regular basis? It may take some experimentation before you find the right one.

2. If you can't locate a local critique group, look for someone in the writing community from whom you can learn. Can you read their communications on a regular basis? Can you touch base with them on email from time to time? What schedule will work for you and this other writer? Like looking for a critique group, you will have to take initiative to create such a situation. Take the first step this week.

CHAPTER 5

Follow the Characteristics of Success

Throughout my writing career, I've written profiles about more than 150 best-selling authors. A small percentage of these authors are rarely interviewed because they don't need publicity for their books to sell. They've reached such a pinnacle in their publishing careers that they are often also involved in radio or television. Thus, whenever they publish a new book, it often appears on the best-seller list because they have a waiting audience.

During one period of my writing, I wrote monthly magazine articles about these authors. I would interview them at bookseller conventions, or in their homes or offices. Some of the information from those interviews was the basis for my published articles. Yet as a writer, I gained much more insight than I was ever able to demonstrate in my articles. From my interaction with these writers, I observed a series of characteristics of successful authors.

In the pages of this chapter, I distill my experiences into a dozen characteristics. Success leaves traces and there are universal attitudes and principles which will help you if you build them into your writing practices. They will move your career into gear and jumpstart your publishing dreams.

1. Writing Is Filled with Large and Small Challenges. Every writing project is filled with problems. As you attempt to write, you will not be immune from difficulties but you need to rise to the challenge and overcome them.

Maybe you are constantly interrupted when you write and struggle to find time for your writing. Successful authors figure out a way to accomplish their writing in spite of other events happening in their lives.

As I've interviewed many well-known and lesser-known writers, I've found that each one has overcome remarkable obstacles in their path and journey. With more than 12 million novels in print, Frank Peretti is nothing short of a publishing phenomenon and has been called "America's hottest Christian novelist." *The Oath* (Word Publishing 1995) sold more than half a million copies within the first six months of release. *The Visitation* (Word Publishing 1999) was #1 on the CBA fiction best-seller list for four months.

Many people do not realize the tragic story of Peretti's injury at birth and how he developed a medical condition called cystic hygroma that nearly killed him. Throughout his childhood, he had repeated surgeries which left him with a tongue that hung out of his mouth, oozing a bloody, blackish residue around his chin and mouth. Peretti's loving family showered him with affection but his wounding began when he attended school. Smaller than many of the other children, he was teased and tormented. When he reached the seventh grade, Frank's tongue continued to stick out of his mouth and he had a speech impediment. He bore a timid personality from the teasing and personal torment of his previous years.

At the "Life on the Edge" seminar sponsored by Focus on the Family, Peretti "spilled his guts." As the final speaker, he didn't get much feedback from the teens but many adults and other speakers told him how the talk touched their lives. "Everyone is carrying a wounded spirit," Frank explained. "At some point in their life, they too have been teased, name called and wounded."

Few people recall the slow success of Peretti's fiction career. He wrote *This Present Darkness* while working at a ski factory in Washington State. The book was rejected 14 times before Crossway Books published it. For the first year and a half, the book had a slow reception then people began to talk about it and the sales figures took off like a rocket. Talking about his writing process, Peretti said, "It takes me about two years to write a novel. I'm kind of a slow writer and I've never been able to write a book faster than that." In preparation, Frank creates a complex outline of his story. Then as he writes, it's like watching a movie in his head. He smiles and says, "I know where I'm going and I know what has to happen, but after that anything else can happen. It's fun to watch."

Peretti advises writers, "If you really want to write, make sure to do it. The most frequent excuse that I hear from people who want to write but aren't writing is that they don't have the time. If you want to be a writer, it has to be important enough that you will make the time to write every day—even if it is just for an hour."

In February 2005, the well-known playwright Arthur Miller died. In 1944, the young Miller wrote a play called "The Man Who Had All the Luck" which closed after only four Broadway performances. As Miller said about his plays, "Every play has a secret. This one has a deep one. It's a combination of fantasy and reality—and you've got to strike the balance just right." An MSNBC story[9] said, "Arthur Miller never stopped writing." His early experience in playwriting could have discouraged him to the point that he quit writing. Instead, he pushed beyond this experience and joined the distinguished group of writers who overcame any challenges in their path. It drove him to write such classic plays as "Death of a Salesman" and "The Crucible."

2. A Little Discipline Goes a Long Way. Each of us flinches a little when we read the word "discipline" because consistency and discipline are a pain. Yet repeatedly I've seen the merit of discipline. I know a best-selling novelist who is also a pastor's wife. When she is facing a novel deadline, she will set her alarm for 3 a.m. so she can have the quiet in her home to write. While we may chaff at this type of discipline to write, it works and is how many writers are successful and prolific.

3. Use the Winning Combination of Persistence and Perseverance. It's easy to look at some best-selling authors and figure they've always had great success. For example, Dan Brown, the author of *The Da Vinci Code* landed in the tenth spot in 2006 on the Forbes 100 list, earning an estimated $88 million—up from the twelfth spot in 2005.[10] Also in 2006, Brown was accused of plagiarism in a London court—which he successfully defended. The 77-page court transcript[11] reveals that he knows and understands the necessity of persistence and perseverance for anyone in publishing.

In the transcript, Brown talks about his journey as a novelist and tells about a period six years earlier in 2000, saying, "This was not an easy time financially. I remember that we were forced to literally sell books out of our car at low profile publishing events. The few readers who read *Angels & Demons* had gone wild for it."

Even in 1998 while writing *Angels & Demons*, Brown was working hard on the promotion of his earlier novel, *Digital Fortress*. His wife,

Blythe, acted as his personal publicist, writing press releases and booking radio show interviews and stories with newspaper reporters. In *The Man Behind the Da Vinci Code, An Unauthorized Biography of Dan Brown*, Lisa Rogak writes,

> Blythe seemingly had her work cut out for her. Most novels are difficult—if not impossible—to promote to the media with press releases and other publicity materials. It's much easier to get the attention of the media by promoting a nonfiction book, particularly a how-to or other prescriptive nonfiction book, because then a publicist can market the title as a solution to a problem…The publicity materials that Blythe developed focused on the scary aspects of what people didn't know about their email. Who's Reading Your E-mail? And Who's Watching You Online? were two angles that made Dan Brown popular with reporters and producers. Some days he would do four radio interviews a day to talk about *Digital Fortress*.[12]

Where are you in the process of pursuing your dreams about publication? It is hard work to make the right pitch with the right book proposal. Many people don't put the energy and effort into their proposal to craft this pitch. Or they send it to the wrong places. Or they give up on the idea too easily. It's a subjective business and you have to tell your story over and over to build enough enthusiasm for it to succeed in the marketplace of ideas.

Why is it so difficult? Statistics repeatedly show that reading statistics are on the decline. Each year about 190,000 new books are published with millions of backlist books already in print (published in the past seasons). If you are feeling low, take smaller steps such as beginning an electronic newsletter and sending it on a regular basis. If you are receiving rejections with your submissions and ideas, continue building relationships with editors and learning your craft. This will take you down the road to achieve your larger dream because you are learning the process and building your publishing credits. Most of all keep holding on to your dreams and working each day to make a difference. You can do it! If you need encouragement, consider the seven-year difference in Dan Brown's life—selling books in the back of his car to #10 on the Forbes 100 list.

4. Find Ways to Celebrate Any Success and Don't Take It for Granted. Find another writer who can share your joy and celebration. It may take some experimentation to find this listening ear, but you need the affirmation—and it will spur you on to even greater achievements.

About fifteen years ago, one of my editors commented on my attitude of celebration with each success saying, "Terry, you act like each publication was your first one." In this case he was criticizing my attitude and I learned not to go to this person to celebrate future milestones. Every article and each book and each online article is significant.

I never want to "assume" my work will be published. I've been around some best-selling authors who take their publication achievements for granted. It's not a pretty picture. I've observed these writers falling off their best-selling status and becoming callous to the spiritual impact of their writing. In my view, they've wandered into dangerous territory and it's something to guard against happening in your own life.

5. Believe in the Quality of Your Work and the Value of Your Message. Every writer needs to take the attitude of a working professional. You want your writing to be accepted and appreciated. To achieve this, you have to produce quality writing. I believe in my own work. My goals are to be clear and tell a good story. I'm not throwing something together in hopes it will be accepted, but I'm crafting each article and each chapter for a book and taking nothing for granted.

In some parts of the writing world I've found people look down their noses at magazines with a small circulation or the few books which come from certain publishers. These people act like these publications are so small that it's "beneath their skills" or second class. Don't accept or absorb such an attitude. Each piece of your writing should be quality writing and also have value for the reader.

6. Learn from Every Possible Source. Good writing can be learned from many different venues, yet one of the keys to application of this principle is your attitude. Successful writers commit to a continual path of growth for their craft. Despite my journalism degree from one of the top schools in the United States, I continue to read at least one how-to-write book each month. One month I will read a book about writing fiction and the next month something relating to query letter writing for magazines. Or I will read a book about improving my marketing skills or any number of other endless possibilities.

Many years ago, I supervised another author who had written at least a dozen books. At that time, I had not written any books and I asked this writer if he ever attended any writer's conferences. I wanted to see if this writer was continuing to grow in his craft. His answer revealed his attitude: "Yes, I go to a conference if I'm invited to teach." For the last fifteen years, I've been teaching at least one conference a year, yet I was disappointed with this author's response. Besides teaching at conferences, I also have been committed to attending at least one a year for my own learning and growth. Take the attitude that you can learn from the newest writer, or the most experienced best-selling author, and you will always be improving your skills for the marketplace.

7. Act Wisely and Thoughtfully. Haste Usually Makes Waste.
One of the publishers where I worked took a nonfiction book from their backlist and gave it a new package with a new cover and new interior type. These types of changes are routine within publishing and often provoke new sales for a book, but in this case it backfired. The busy editors didn't keep a watchful eye on the new look for the interior as the book quickly went through the publishing process. The printed book was riddled with typographical errors. Suddenly a project that was supposed to be simple became complex because the supply chain for the book was disrupted. The new version was destroyed since it would only provoke complaints from readers and a

revised version was printed. While the error was fixed, the book was temporarily out of print.

Repeatedly within publishing, I've seen this characteristic in practical application. When something is rushed through the publishing system, it usually results in errors. I understand some projects require a rushed deadline, but you should consider the consequences when you are involved in these efforts.

8. Never Resist Rewriting. Your Words Are Not Etched in Stone. I opened the letter from the magazine editor and read it a second time. I was angry about what it contained. Writing on assignment, I had put together a service article for the magazine and the editor did not like several details about how my story was put together. In fact, he asked me to rewrite the article and gave me a new deadline. I groaned as I thought about the additional work. It is a typical reaction to react negatively to an editor's instructions. Then I remembered that the editor is the guardian of the publication for his or her readers. More than anyone else, they know what the readers need and are the quality control experts. After a brief period of fuming, I returned to my keyboard and wrote what the editor requested. Professional writers need to be willing to rewrite or adjust their material to the needs of the publication and follow the editor's instructions.

Some writers will fight to prevent any changes in their manuscript and this word gets around to other editors and publishing houses. The attitude of the professional writer is to be cooperative and work with the editor to make any changes to the manuscript with the focus on the overall good of the project. If someone wants me to improve a story through rewriting, I've learned to always be glad to do it. As I admitted, I may go into my office and mutter to myself, but then I will complete the task as the editor requested because I know it *always* turns out for the best.

9. Never Resist Editing Because Again Your Words Are Not Etched in Stone. Magazine editors tend to move fairly rapidly. Sometimes as a part of their procedure, they don't send you the edited version of your story. Long ago, a magazine editor told me that any changes to my story should be subtle and barely recognizable. Good editors will maintain the writer's original tone and flavor; others will rewrite large sections of the article as a part of the editorial process. Only a few times have I complained about an editor's work on my magazine article or my book manuscript as I understand the responsibility of an editor is to produce the best possible work in the allowed time frame. If you are going to complain about the editing of your work, make sure you carefully evaluate whether this battle is worth fighting. Ask yourself several key questions:

- If I complain or make alternative suggestions, is there time in the schedule for these changes to be easily made in the printed book or magazine?

- If it is too late, what will my complaint do to my relationship with this editor and will it damage any potential for future work? You may win the battle but lose the war.

Your answers to these questions will affect whether you complain about the editing or not. In the majority of cases, you will probably let it go—at least that is how I have reacted over the years. The majority of these battles are not worth the fight.

10. Understand the Power of Relationships and Keeping Track. For almost 20 years of my writing life, I've been automatically updating information such as addresses, phone numbers, and email addresses. It doesn't take a great deal of time but it's a consistent and conscious act on my part.

I know some of the data in my computer rolodex is a bit dated. Yet I keep it there because sometimes even an out-of-date address has value. Several years ago as an acquisitions editor, the managing editor turned a project over to me. This author who has a busy counseling ministry owed the publisher a manuscript. There had been some back and forth email correspondence to talk about the editorial details with this manuscript. When I took the background information including the book contract from my colleague, I asked, "What's a current phone number for this author?"

The managing editor replied, "I've never talked with him on the phone. We've only communicated through email." Heading back to my desk, I knew I needed to reach this author on the phone and talk through these editorial issues. Email has its purpose—but it's also a less personal means of reaching someone. It's pretty easy to turn someone down via email or reshape their request or idea. I knew on the phone and in person, the conversation would be much more ground leveling with this best-selling author. But where do I find the phone number since it wasn't in the file?

About fifteen years earlier, I had worked with this author as an editor and ghostwriter on one of his books. During that brief experience, we communicated a great deal but I hadn't talked with him in years, yet his old information remained in my rolodex. It was a starting point. I called the old phone numbers and they didn't work. My only choice was the front door approach. I called this author's office and reached his assistant. When I explained the need, this assistant said, "You could be anyone on the phone, Terry, posing as a publisher. I can't give you that information."

I tried a different tact, "Does he still live in (name of the city), California?"

"Yes."

"Does he live at (specific street address)?"

"Yes."

"Is his old home phone number (specific area code and number)?"

After giving this information, the assistant made a long pause on the phone. Then with a sigh, she said, "Yes, that's the phone number but the area code has changed to ____." I thanked her for her "assistance." In a matter of minutes I was talking with this author's wife (another bit of information in my rolodex) and beginning to connect with him about my editorial issue. I understand the power of keeping track.

What do you do after you get someone's business card? Toss it on your desk or put it in your computer where you can easily access it? For many years, I keyed the information from my business cards into my computer rolodex. I understand the power of such information—even if it's old.

11. Treat Editors As the Coach on Your Team. They know their audience so respect their counsel and only reject it with good reason. Often in films and books and other media, editors are characterized as the enemy to the writer. It's not true. The editor is the best ally you can have so you want to treat them as colleagues. You are teammates, not adversaries. Adopting this attitude will increase your longevity in the marketplace.

12. Never Rest on Your Laurels. Always be on the lookout for your next opportunity. To have your work printed in a magazine or a book is a great victory which should be celebrated—at least for a few minutes. Then look for your next project. If you want to build longevity in the market, always be looking toward the future.

Some Final Encouragement

Some authors are a flash in the marketplace. Their books appear and it is the only book they ever write and manage to get published. These characteristics of success are for the long haul. If you build them into your writing life, they will position you as a professional who has a long-range vision for working in the publishing community.

Dig Deeper

1. Read *Stein on Writing* by Sol Stein. (St. Martin's Press, 1995) This book contains timeless wisdom and instruction. A New York publisher for 27 years and the author of a million-copy bestseller, Stein is a master editor and writing coach for some of the most successful writers in our century. This title contains wonderful insight on fiction or nonfiction.

2. Read books like *The Man Behind the Da Vinci Code*—and learn from the experiences of other writers. Zero in on profiles in magazines and newspapers and draw from the experiences of others.

Awaken Your Dreams

1. Return to these characteristics. Take active steps to build more of them into your own writing life.

2. Which of these characteristics in particular can you focus on? Create a specific plan for your own growth.

CHAPTER 6

Move from Idea to Article

Over the last 10 to 15 years, though books have been my passion and represent the bulk of my writing life, it's not where I began. Please don't misunderstand. I love books but I continue to believe many writers are missing golden opportunities by not practicing the short form—magazine writing.

In the article format, I'm able to practice many of the techniques I use in my books, but in a more condensed form. It's a sharpening process for my writing life and important. If you are writing books exclusively, I recommend you return to writing magazine articles. It will build something into your books.

In this chapter, I'm going to provide specific insight into each step of the magazine writing process. Where do you get ideas? How do you pitch these ideas to the editor in a query letter? How do you find people to interview? How do you interview? After the interview, how do you write the article?

I'll be walking you through the specifics and hopefully providing some tips for you—whether you are just starting the process or have written hundreds of articles and several books.

The Idea Factory

Ideas are one of the most fluid and freewheeling parts of the writing process. I love new ideas—and they come constantly. Sometimes the waves of what I want to write spring into my mind so fast, it's like standing under a waterfall. You can't possibly catch everything—and like a waterfall you can only stand the spray for a tiny bit before you get washed away.

Conversations with people can stir ideas. You may be taking a break at work and listening to someone's story and decide an altered version of the story could be part of a novel. Or you see your friend struggling with a personal crisis and discovering a unique solution. You decide that experience could be the beginnings of a how-to article. I've given only two examples of how we can find ideas from our conversations with others.

Other times we read the newspaper and learn about a unique product. Because we read magazines and other types of print or Internet publications, the idea comes to write about this product. You take this idea, pitch a magazine, and snag an assignment. Reading stimulates your idea process. Can you take the idea, twist it in a different fashion, and reveal the product or service to a new audience and a different publication?

Years ago, I was living in Southern California and was reading the Orange County Register. In the business section, a small news item announced that Disney was printing Disney Dollars which had the same value as regular currency. I was fascinated with this bit of news and wanted to learn more. I pitched a numismatic magazine with the article idea and received an assignment. In a matter of weeks, I was on the back lot of Disney where no "guests" are allowed, and interviewing one of the vice presidents about this new currency. For me the process began with an item in the newspaper. You can find ideas the same way.

Almost anything can stir ideas—family activities, walking through the mall, visiting a historic monument or you name it. I've learned to always carry a piece of paper because ideas strike me at odd times. If I don't write them down, they will pass through my mind and be forgotten. (In general, I ignore the ones that come in the middle of the night.)

Now that you have an idea, what do you do with it? This is the key to whether you get it published or let it disappear. Does the idea drive you wild? Does it drive you to begin researching or writing an article? The experience doesn't always have to be dramatic. Yet occasionally this is the case. You have to find a piece of paper or get to your computer and begin writing. If you've not done much writing for magazines (or even if you have done it), it's perfectly OK to write the entire article—as long as you keep several things in mind:

- Always keep the reader firmly in your mind. What will they take away from your article?

- Who is the potential market for the article? Where will you submit it? Some publications read full manuscripts while others will read only query letters.

- The most likely possibilities for magazines are ones that you read often and are intimately familiar with their contents and their readers (since you are one).

- Keep in mind the standard length for these target publications. It will not help you to write 3,000 words if the guidelines ask for 1,000 words. In general, magazines are using shorter articles.

- Magazines generally plan their content about four to six months ahead of their publication date. For example if you have a Valentine's Day experience you want to write, you should submit it before September 1st.

There are several different types of magazine articles, one of the strongest being the personal experience article. The story is written in first person and you tell your personal experience in such a way that you have a single key point or takeaway for the reader. Other types of articles include service articles (to promote or tell about a new consumer product or service), how-to articles (how to make something or do some activity), personality profile articles (often focused on a well-known person or someone who has an interesting life or life experience), "as told to" articles (where you write in the first person tense of another person and write their story) and the celebrity interviews (often done on assignment—more about this later).

Your enthusiasm carries you to move ahead and get your thoughts on paper. Next, you channel your enthusiasm about the idea into a one-page letter called a query.

Most of the higher paying magazines prefer to receive this single-page pitch letter. Within a few minutes, the editor can determine if the idea is appropriate for their publication. Because of the volume of submissions, many editors will not respond unless the answer is positive. It's one of those reality checks writers need to hear.

You aren't looking for a "no, thank you." You are looking for an assignment or a "go ahead" or a "yes" response from the editor. Writing an effective query letter is one of the most important skills for you to develop. As you write these letters, you will refine and improve your technique. I recommend Lisa Collier Cool's excellent book, *Irresistible Query Letters* (Writer's Digest Books).

I prefer writing on assignment. You can also snag assignments as you learn to write a riveting query letter that will entice the editor to pick up the phone and call you for more information. Or you want that editor to open an email and write you immediately asking when you can send a completed manuscript. I hope you can see the importance of this skill as a writer.

With increased publishing experience, you can expect to write more on assignment and less on speculation ("spec"). Even an assigned piece can sometimes not work out for a particular publication, however. Maybe the editor thought the query was a good idea, but the execution was wrong for their publication. I've not had this experience often but it does happen. In these cases, the magazine will often pay a "kill fee"—a token payment for the work you poured into the article. This is better than nothing, but is still pretty disappointing.

Just remember, on the road to publication there are many possible junctures where you can fail. Some factors are in your control and others are not. Let's say you have your magazine idea and hopefully an assignment from your query letter. What resources do you need to write this article? Will it involve research at the library or online?

Will you need to interview someone for the article? How do you snag an interview with an expert? It's easier than you would initially imagine. Has this "expert" written a book? Then your best course of action is to call the publisher and ask to speak to someone in publicity. (It's one of the few times I recommend people call the publisher.) Tell the publicist about your assignment and ask for background materials (review copies of the books, other articles, etc.).

Then ask the publicist to set up your interview and give the person the times you are available.

Wise authors who want to sell books take advantage of these interview possibilities. You will quote this "expert," mention their book in the article, and get to tap their expertise for your article. It works as a package and everyone gains from the experience—you, the expert, and the publisher.

For more than 20 years, I've been interviewing people. Some of them are well-known celebrities and best-selling authors, others are unknown. No matter who I'm interviewing, I get a touch of panic right before the interview happens. Maybe it's the same sort of adrenaline rush that I've read about in sports. I'm hesitant to admit it but it still happens. I then go about the interview in a professional manner, and whether well-known or unknown, each of these people have graciously answered my questions and provided the story material I've needed for my magazine articles.

Whether you interview on the telephone or in person, it's an excellent skill for every writer to add to their professional experiences. For beginning writers, I recommend you begin with someone familiar—such as a family member or a friend. Prepare a list of questions, establish a time, and turn on your recorder. I recommend recording the interview so you can capture the quotations and don't always have to be tied to writing notes. I've never been able to write fast enough (even though I learned shorthand in high school) to capture someone talking at a regular pace. It slows down the interview process to continually pause, and it's awkward for the person to wait as you complete your notes. I record to make sure I get my quotations right, and as protection if the interviewee later claims they were misquoted.

If you are recording on the telephone, I recommend you use the Radio Shack "Smart" Phone Recorder Control. For legal reasons, most states require that you tell the other person that you are recording and secure their permission on the recording. This device makes recording easy because it's directly connected from your telephone line into any recorder. Telephone interviews are some of the most difficult—because you can't see the other person for the visuals to add to the article. Also, it's a situation much more out of your control. For example, the other person can have an interruption and suddenly need to end the conversation. Then you are left without the required information.

Whether on the phone or in person, make sure you prepare with a list of questions, allowing time, however, for other questions that may arise during the interview. Like many of the skills, interviewing is something to practice repeatedly so your techniques will improve.

Over the years, I've been amazed at the people who forget about my recorder and say to me, "I've never told this to anyone but..." Often this material becomes some of the best in my articles.

During the interview, I always make a note how to contact the person for possible follow-up questions or to give them a copy of the article. In general, the higher profile the person, the more typical it is for them to call you—and not reveal their phone number—often for control purposes.

Another option is the email interview. Several years ago, a magazine assigned me to write a story which was printed just before the release of *Glorious Appearing* in the Left Behind series (which has sold over 60 million books). My editor wanted me to interview retailers, along with some people from Tyndale House Publishers, plus the authors. The last person on the interview list proved to be my greatest challenge. I've known Jerry B. Jenkins, the writer, for more than 20 years and he graciously gave some time for the short interview.

I could not wrangle an interview time with Tim LaHaye, however, despite years in this business and the fact that I've interviewed more than 150 best-selling authors over the years. My last resort was an email interview with him. I submitted my questions ahead of time and then waited for a response. Thankfully it came before my deadline and I was able to include some of the material in my article. As a journalist, it's an unsatisfactory experience to interview someone via email and it should be used only as the last possible option. It's not something I recommend writers use for several reasons:

- The interview is totally outside of your control in the information you gather.

- The person you are interviewing via email might never answer your email or send his response after your deadline.

- There is no opportunity for follow-up questions or clarification or immediate insight. Yes, you can send a follow-up email, but again you abdicate (yes a strong word) your role as the writer to the person you are interviewing. You essentially transfer control of the interview to them.

Some of my best magazine articles came from a follow-up question when I was personally interviewing someone. The questions may not have been on my prepared list but they were asked and brought out some fascinating details. It happens both on the telephone (my least favorite medium) and in person (my recommended choice for interviews if at all possible).

Let's also examine this question from the role of the person being interviewed via email:

- They will answer the questions, but at their own convenience.

- I've been "interviewed" via email several times and I find the experience creates a lot of extra work for me—and I'm a writer. Imagine it for a person who doesn't like to write. How do they handle it? Or do they just skip it?

Yes, it takes time and energy to set up face-to-face interviews or telephone interviews. But the payoff from these types of interviews is better and more accurate information than email interviews for your magazine article plus you have opportunity for a give-and-take interaction. In a face-to-face interview you can also jot down information on the surroundings, gestures, dress, and facial expressions.

Only use the email interview as your last possible resort. You are working hard to write a magazine article targeted for a particular publication. How you put together the specific article will depend on the particular audience. No matter which type of magazine article you are writing, you always need to keep the reader in mind. Not to focus on the reader is a common mistake that many unpublished or even experienced writers make with their magazine writing.

You've accomplished your research and your interviews for the article. What next? Do you transcribe your interview recording? At one of the publications where I worked, we were required to transcribe any interview. It's common for me to record my interviews, but I have learned not to take the time to transcribe the recording because it puts the words in stone—firmly fixed. Writing is a fluid process and you need to have the freedom to move the quotations and information around from an interview to shape the best possible article. I listen to my recording to verify the quotations and make sure I have the details from the personal interview, but I do not transcribe them.

With the various pieces of information, I create a brief outline of the entire article including subheads—short headlines that break up the text. This makes it more inviting to today's reader and the editor will appreciate your efforts in this area. How will your article begin? With a provocative question? A stirring quotation? A startling fact? A riveting story? There are many possibilities. Also how will your article end? What will be the takeaway?

In this chapter, I've only scratched the surface of the magazine article creation process. I hope I have stirred some help for you in this area.

Dig Deeper

Here are three books on magazine writing that I recommend you locate and carefully read:

• *The Magazine Article, How to Think It, Plan It, Write It* by Peter Jacobi (Indiana University Press, 1997) www.snipurl.com/themagart. Dr. Jacobi regularly teaches at Folio seminars which is where editors of the major magazines get additional training.

• *Basic Magazine Writing* by Barbara Kevles (Writer's Digest Books, 1986). This book covers seven different types of articles.

• *Handbook of Magazine Article Writing* (Writer's Digest Books, 1990). This volume contains a compilation of some of the best articles about magazine writing from past issues of *Writer's Digest* magazine.

Awaken Your Dreams

1. After reading this chapter, I hope you are more confident about the process of writing for magazines. Write down three publications that you would like to approach with an idea over the next few weeks.

2. Create an action plan to craft query letters for each of these publications and give yourself a specific deadline to mail these letters.

CHAPTER 7

Celebrate the Value of Reading

As a former literary agent and now an acquisition editor, I've had the privilege of participating on the faculty of a number of writer's conferences throughout the United States and Canada. One of the key benefits to attending a conference is to meet with the editor face-to-face and pitch an idea for your book. I've been in hundreds of these 15-minute one-on-one meetings with writers. In this brief period of time, an editor learns about the book but it's also an opportunity for that editor or agent to ask a couple of key questions. On a regular basis I will ask the writer about their motivation to write the book they are presenting to me.

Why? If you have written a novel or a nonfiction book, I want to see your passion about your topic and your book. From my years in the marketplace, I know there are many obstacles to writing books and your passion will carry you through many of these obstacles. The majority of the time I meet with writers, a portion of their motivation comes from their own reading habits. For example, readers of romance novels enjoy writing this type of book, while history buffs may write historical fiction.

Occasionally my questions reveal that the writer does not read in the area where they want to write. For me, this shows they are disconnected from their subject and gives me a bit of caution as I read their material. If you have read hundreds of romance novels, in addition to developing a love of the genre, you have internalized many of the writing patterns of these books. You have not gone through this process if you haven't devoted the energy to reading in the genre in which you want to publish.

Sometimes when I ask a writer why she has devoted the writing time and energy to produce an 80,000-word manuscript in an unfamiliar field, I will hear something like, "I read a few of them and thought they were fun so I tried it."

As a writer, you can use your own reading habits to guide you into the area you want to be published. Nine biographies on people like Billy Graham and Chuck Colson are among my list of published books. Also I've profiled the personal stories of more than 150 best-selling authors in various magazines. I can attribute some of my abilities in this area directly to the reading patterns of my youth.

Many summers my younger sister and I would spend at our granny's home in Frankfort, Kentucky. We spent a lot of time outdoors but I also spent a good portion of time curled up with a library book. The Frankfort library was within walking distance of my grandmother's home so I would walk there and check out a stack of biographies. In my mind's eye, I can still clearly see the red and yellow hard-covered books bearing the names of United States presidents or historical figures or sports heroes. I would check out five or six of these books, carry them home, and read one after another throughout the summer.

I did not care about a particular author; rather, I was focused on reading biographies about a particular person's life and experiences. My hours of reading these books built something significant into my own life and they continue to affect the book-length projects that draw my attention as a writer today.

Readers love words. When you can find a quiet moment, do you curl up with a good book? I love a great story for a bit of escape. Also I love to learn new thoughts or a new skill with a good nonfiction book. The world includes both. Which type of book do you read and why?

Through the years, I have spent a lot of time poring over books. You can gain amazing insight as you learn from the experience of others. For over 20 years, I've made a commitment to read at least one how-to book about writing each month; often it's more. The five-shelf bookcase in my office is jammed with writing books that contain a wealth of information. They are not just decorations, but are read and highlighted and, in some cases, re-read. Your own reading patterns will be indicators of the type of publishing on which you can focus your attention and efforts.

"I'm a librarian, not a search engine."

The Amazing Smell

I've never been much of a shopper or someone who loves to wander around malls looking at the various stores. There is one exception to this tendency, I love bookstores. During a recent visit as I walked into a Barnes and Noble bookstore, the scent of new books struck me. It's as though the ink was barely dry on those pages.

As I look around a bookstore, I try and gather much more information than the average bookstore browser. I'm always interested to see which books are close to the front door of the store and especially the books near the cash register. I take a look at the bestsellers and, in particular, any books recently released or discussed in *Publishers Weekly*, a trade magazine for the publishing world, or other publications that I read.

If nonfiction, I look to see who wrote it and if the person is a celebrity or someone else with high visibility. If fiction, I will often open the book and read the first few pages to see if I'm drawn into the story.

Toward the back of Barnes and Noble, in a prominent position, is a large rack of classic books such as *Little Women* or *Jane Eyre* or *Robinson Crusoe*. If you notice, these books have redesigned covers and a modern appearance. Why? As classics they have stood the test of time. People read these books year after year and use them in their book groups and education classes.

In addition, as I wander around the bookstore, I'm always interested in books marked "bargain" or "reduced." These books have been remaindered; the price has been lowered intentionally to sell whatever copies the publisher has stored in their warehouse. Look closely at these books because they are on their final trip in front of the buying public. After a certain number of days or weeks, if these books do not sell, then the bookstore returns them to the publisher for a full refund and they are destroyed. Notice the copyright date on these books and how the retail price has been drastically reduced to entice a quick sale.

I also use my brief time in a bookstore to collect information about what people are buying, how the books are displayed, and how they are marketed to the public. And I'm always interested in the design of the best-selling fiction and nonfiction books. There are many ways to purchase books online and also other methods, but for me, I look forward to going in the bookstore, holding the books, and looking at them firsthand. From my years in this business I know that writers are readers. I enjoyed my recent Saturday afternoon outing to the bookstore. If nothing else, I will be returning for that amazing smell.

Reading Adjusts Your Attitude

While I love to read and it is a familiar pattern in my life, I understand that I'm an exception to the bulk of those people around me. The amount of time spent reading continues to decline with each study. For example a 2007 study from the National Endowment for the Arts found, "Americans are reading less—teens and young adults read less often and for shorter amounts of time compared with other age groups and with Americans of previous years."[13] It is just one more indicator that people are spending their time watching television, playing video games, or playing on their computers instead of reading a book.

One of the keys when it comes to reading is your own attitude. Are you making it a priority in your life? In *Marketing Is King*, Ali Pervez encourages a workable plan:

> Never miss your fifteen minutes of reading per day. As Jim Rohn, the famous motivational speaker says, "Miss a meal, but don't miss your daily reading." This will give you over one and a half hours of mental exercise per week!

Remember what you put in your mind will eventually show itself. So be careful what gets in! Inspirational reading is food for the mind![14]

In 1981, best-selling novelist Dean R. Koontz published a how-to book called *How to Write Bestselling Fiction* which has been out of print for many years. Whenever I find a used copy for sale, it often has a large price tag like $250. This book is packed with sound advice, but I especially love the final chapter called, "Read, read, read or Read, read, read," Which lists contemporary mainstream novelists. As Koontz says,

> The more you broaden your interest as a reader, the more you will simultaneously broaden your perspective and your talent as a writer. I know a few authors who read only one kind of fiction, the kind they write themselves; in every case, this provincialism is evident in the author's work, and none of these writers is very successful in the marketplace.[15]

He concludes his introduction in this chapter by saying, "Once you have read the people I recommend, for God's sake don't stop! Your need to read some fiction every day should be almost like a drug dependency. Read, read, read!"[16] From his passionate review of modern-day fiction, it is obvious that Koontz follows his own directions. It's a pattern as a writer that you can learn from and emulate in your own life.

My Newspaper Habit

Some habits are worth keeping while others should be abandoned. One long-term habit that feeds into my writing and editing life is my love of the local newspaper. My personal love affair with the newspaper started in high school when I began working part-time at the local *Peru Tribune* in Peru, Indiana and expanded during my college journalism training as a newspaper journalist. Ralph Holsinger, former editor at *The Cincinnati Enquirer*, taught an advanced reporting/editing class which was one of the required journalism classes. For this course, each day we were required to read several national newspapers, along with the local campus newspaper. When you entered Mr. Holsinger's classroom, you had to be prepared for one of his pop quizzes which included specific questions such as "Where is Vice President Agnew *today*?" (Now you know the era I was in college.) As young reporters, we learned to collect these types of details and file them away. It's a habit that has stuck with me for over 20 years.

Personally, I love the feel of newsprint and glean a great deal of information from the newspaper. I love to read about my local environment and the newspaper is often a breeding ground for story ideas, insight and leads. When I travel, I read the local newspaper and, depending on the location, a national newspaper. Each spring when I attend the American Society of Journalists and Authors' conference, I love to read *The New York Times*. The newspaper habit has been an important one for my writing and editing life, and it's one that I'm determined to keep.

I'm a reader—newspapers, magazines, books, whatever. You name it and I'll be reading it. Maybe it's the way I'm wired. As I process a great deal of information, details begin to come together and stick out. It's a practice I recommend to others. Another area where I regularly read is trade magazines such as *Publisher's Weekly*. I may not read every single detail in every article but I do pick up on a large portion of this publication and try to carefully evaluate what I'm reading. You never know how these different details will come together into something significant in your daily work. It happens in my writing and editing life all the time.

Each issue of *Publishers Weekly* highlights a different aspect of publishing. One week, it emphasizes comic books; another week cookbooks, biographies, or reference books. With the various genres of books, the possibilities are almost endless and each type of book has its own news and distinctions.

From reading this chapter, hopefully you can understand the necessity that every writer who wants to be published needs to continually emphasize reading. It will enrich your life and strengthen your writing.

Dig Deeper

1. Two books on my shelf celebrate the value of reading. *You've GOT To Read This Book, 55 People Tell the Story of the Book That Changed Their Life* by Jack Canfield and Gay Hendricks (Collins Living, 2007), and *A Passion for Books* by Terry W. Glaspey (Harvest House, 1998). Locate one of these books and dig deeper into the topic of how reading affects people's lives.

Awaken Your Dreams

1. What types of books do you enjoy reading? Do those books fall into a particular genre of writing? Can you use this experience to help guide you into fulfilling your own publishing dreams?

2. When you shop for a new book to read, what draws your attention—the first few pages of a novel, the author, or the story? Think about what draws you as a consumer and it will help you be in touch with this information for your own writing project.

CHAPTER 8

Strengthen Your Storytelling with Interviews

My nerves were on edge with anticipation about my forthcoming interview. I had tested my recorder and it was ready to use. In front of me, I had my prepared list of questions which I had reviewed and I was ready. Now, in anticipation of the call, I paced the floor of my two-bedroom apartment to calm my nerves as I got ready for one of the highest profile interviews of my career.

In the middle of a presidential election year, I had snagged an interview with the current vice president of the United States, Dan Quayle, who was running for president. Weeks earlier, I had pitched a magazine and been assigned a cover story for a November issue. The vice president's publisher, Zondervan, understood the significance of such a cover story so they convinced Mr. Quayle to agree to my interview request. According to my publicist contact at Zondervan, my interview was one of only two or three that the vice president agreed to fit into his busy schedule to promote his new book.

Typical for these types of high-profile interviews, they requested a list of my questions in advance so the subject feels more prepared. I complied with their request, crafted a list of questions, and sent them through the publicist. Notice that I did not have a direct connection to the vice president but I worked through the book publisher. Communication difficulty increases as you are distanced from the person that you are interviewing but there wasn't anything I could do about this situation except work through the publisher which was my connection to the Vice President.

Finally my interview was confirmed and set up for a specific time of day. The amount of time for the interview is always negotiated. From experience, I have learned the challenges of a 20 to 30-minute interview because you often can't get beyond the expected answers and surface questions in that short span of time. The person you are interviewing has to take time to form their relationship with you, warm up to their topic, and then begin to tell you something new and fresh. I had pushed for the maximum amount of time with the vice president and managed to get a commitment for a 40-minute interview.

With about 150,000 readers, this magazine wanted the article in a question and answer format which meant they would use the actual conversation of our interview. If the article is written in a storytelling format, you have more flexibility to add details about the book or other background information. This option was eliminated with the Q & A format and increased the pressure on me for a great interview.

Now my interview time had arrived but my phone was not ringing. For the few times I've interviewed anyone in the high-profile category, I rarely had a phone number to initiate the call. Instead they call you at the appropriate time to keep their phone numbers private, and also, to control when the call is made and the length of the interview.

I felt somewhat helpless in this situation but I was thrilled to have one of the few interviews on his schedule. I kept looking over at my telephone, almost willing it to ring. It was silent as I continued to pace the floor of my apartment, check and double-check my equipment and wait for the call. With each tick of the clock, my tension increased as my interview time was slipping away.

Finally the phone rang but it was not Vice President Quayle. One of his assistants identified himself and apologized that the vice president was running late but he affirmed that I was still on the schedule and that he would be calling me soon. I thanked him and before I could ask if I would receive my full 40-minute interview in light of the delay, the assistant said good-bye and hung up.

The hands of my watch continued to move and I rechecked my list of questions and stared at my phone to see when it would ring again. Another ten or fifteen minutes crept past as I wondered if the interview was going to happen.

The phone rang again and the voice on the line was Quayle. With his permission, I activated my recorder and quickly began the interview. I asked if he had my list of questions.

"Yes I have them right here," he said, "But there are a lot of questions. Let's not stick to these. Ask anything you want."

I began to ask my questions and as I expected, I received standard and expected answers to most of them. After about ten minutes and four or five of my questions, the vice president began to conclude each of his answers with, "And is that it? Is that all?"

What do you mean? I thought. *I'm just getting started on my 40-minute interview.* I rapidly fired a couple of additional questions and received some more standard answers which lacked anything original. After three or four answers with the implication that it was the last question, the vice president explained it was all the time that he had. He said good-bye and disconnected the call. I looked at my watch and noted I had spent a total of about 15 minutes in conversation. As I clicked off my recorder, I knew instinctively that my cover story had been killed. Over the next few days, I transcribed my interview and tried to craft it into the required magazine article. Yet when I sent it to my editor, I knew it fell short of their expectations for a cover story. The editor asked for my actual interview recording so I made a copy and sent it to them, waiting several weeks for an answer. Ultimately I got a brief letter saying the story would not be used, and enclosed was a $75 kill fee. My cover story with Vice President Dan Quayle vanished. Through the years, I've conducted thousands of interviews in person and on the telephone and, thankfully, they rarely ended up like my vice president interview.

Another time the editor of *Charisma* magazine called and asked me to write a story about Bishop Phillip Porter, leading African-American in the Promise Keepers organization. I agreed to write the story and arranged to meet Bishop Porter at his church in Denver. From the instant I walked into his office, I could sense a special connection with this gray-haired jovial pastor. During our interview, he confided he had recently signed his first book contract with Creation House and then he said, "Maybe you can be my ghostwriter, Terry."

"Maybe," I replied and made a note about his signed book contract without a writer. When I got home to my office in Colorado Springs, I called the editorial director at that publisher and introduced myself, and then suggested that I become the writer for this project. A simple magazine article led to several books and a long-term relationship with this Christian leader. You never know what can result from an interview. The possibilities are endless if you are open to them.

Over the years, I've written hundreds of magazine articles and conducting an interview is one of the foundational skills for anyone who wants to be published. Yes, you can write stories from your own personal experiences but you can broaden the possibilities for your writing if you learn how to interview and ask questions. The experience of interviewing others will teach you many surprising things about people.

For example, I once interviewed marriage expert Gary Smalley and he told me his snoring had grown so loud that he and his wife, Norma, were sleeping in separate bedrooms. When I heard it, I said, "Gary, time out. You mean the marriage expert isn't sleeping in the same bed as his wife?" The doctor had diagnosed Gary with sleep apnea and eventually, with some changes in his life, he has returned to sleeping in the same bed as his wife. The story was fascinating and when printed, it was called Sleepless in Branson (as in Missouri where Smalley lives). It was the result of a series of prepared interview questions.

If you are going to interview anyone, your preparation is critical to your success. In advance of the appointment, learn as much as you can about the subject through magazine articles and online interviews. If the person has published a book, ask the publicist at the book company to send you copies of any background material, including the author's books. Take the time to read this material in advance of your meeting with the person.

Absorbing this background will help you craft a series of questions which will move beyond the usual facts and stories. I guarantee if you take this step you will produce a better interview and gain improved quality material you need to write your story. As I've interviewed various authors, I've seen relief pass across their face when they realize from my questions that I've read and thought about the contents of their book. It takes time to prepare for interviews, but there is a huge payoff with the subject of your story.

Occasionally a story will require interviewing more than one person and those interviews don't have to be very long. Even ten minutes on the telephone can get some useful stories and quotations, provided you're asking the right questions.

Additional Pointers for Interviewing

- Interviewing is a skill that can be developed. The more you interview people for articles, the better you will be at asking specific and unusual questions. The practice will improve your skills.

- No matter how famous the person, don't forget they are a real person with feelings and concerns. It will help you treat them naturally.

- Whether you interview in person or on the telephone, I recommend you record the interview. First, however, ask for permission to start the recording and get their recorded consent. With this permission, anything that is said is possible material for your article. I prefer to interview someone face-to-face because you can also capture their facial expressions and details about their environment, but this isn't always possible, so be prepared to interview on the telephone.

- When you have an assignment to interview an author, you can often get the interview through the publishing house. The publicist will be eager to get exposure for their books. Build solid relationships with these publicists as they can open doors of opportunity for you to interview well-known people for magazine articles. Most publishers will furnish you with complimentary books as background for your research and schedule the interview time. After the article is published, send, or arrange for the magazine to send, a copy of the article to the publisher. Publicists for publishing houses have dozens of projects going simultaneously. Your article will appear months after you set up the interview. You want to establish your track record with the publishers, and this step of sending them the article builds your credibility and reputation as a writer for future writing projects.

For the Difficult Interview

If you are interviewing a difficult subject, you may be stumped about what to ask. In an article in the *New York Times*, Barbara Walters revealed these five "foolproof" questions for the over-interviewed:

1. If you were recuperating in a hospital, who would you want in the bed next to you, excluding relatives?

2. What was your first job?

3. When was the last time you cried?

4. Who was the first person you ever loved?

5. What has given you the most pleasure in the last year?

No questions are really foolproof and even these questions may backfire. You should ask each one with sensitivity. For example, not everyone will like the hypothetical element in the first question and some people will refuse to speculate with this question.

For any interview, the key ingredient is your personal relationship with the subject. Look for ways to bond and build trust with the person and they will soon open up to you and tell you amazing stories. I've had it happen over and over in my writing life.

As I complete my interview, I am still talking with that person right up until the last moment. Be prepared because often they will say something memorable in those final seconds. It's not unusual for me to restart my recorder and ask them to repeat what they've just said on the recording. Or if that is awkward, I will say good-bye, slip around the corner, and quickly write it down while the words are still ringing in my ears. Sometimes the absolute best information is gathered in those final moments with the subject.

After the Interview—What Now?

After I've hung up the telephone or walked away from a personal interview, my first action is to check my recording. Did it work? Over the years, I've made every possible mistake. I've had the batteries quit working part way through the interview. I've forgotten and left the recorder on pause or hold and not recorded a single word. In the old tape recorder days, I've tried to play the tape and had it crinkle in the recorder and it is ruined. If you face one of these situations, the first rule is not to panic.

While I always record my interviews, I also take notes. I don't get everything but I get the main points on paper. If something has gone wrong, then I get to my computer and write the story as quickly as possible and include the various quotations in my writing. In these moments, I'm grateful for my old journalism training where we had to quickly write stories and get our thoughts on paper. My point is to encourage you not to be overly concerned if something does go wrong but to carve out some immediate writing time to capture the story while it is fresh in your mind.

Even when I check the recorder and it performed without any difficulty (which is 99.9 percent of the time), I attempt to write the story fairly soon after the interview. I will often take the various points from the interview and craft a brief outline, and then write the story from my outline.

I've emphasized the importance of building a relationship with the subject of your interview. Now I'm going to give you another method to build this relationship after the interview. During the interview, if possible, I suggest a way to check the finished article with the subject. I'm careful to say that I'm looking for accuracy and that I want to double check and make sure the quotations are accurate from our session together. In a "pre-publication review," I allow the subjects of my interview to read and comment on the accuracy of the story before it is published.

This practice is contrary to what is taught in journalism schools. We were taught never to let the subject review your article because then you have lost your objectivity. But if you don't do this, and wrong facts are printed, you have damaged your relationship with this person. They will then be hesitant to grant a request for a second story. Send them the article, giving them a time frame to review it and return it to you. From my experience, they will only change a few words and you will have preserved and strengthened your relationship with that subject in case you have the opportunity to interview them again or work with them in any capacity.

Is there mail on a Sunday?

What in the world? I wondered as I walked outside to pick up my Sunday newspaper. A large white package was perched on top of my mailbox. When my regular mail arrived, the package wasn't there. I suspect the package was delivered to the wrong house and someone dropped it off on my box. In any case, I was glad to see it and instantly knew what was inside.

Several months earlier, I was assigned to write a lengthy story for *Sports Spectrum*. It took a number of calls and emails to line up that interview with Shane Doan, captain of the Phoenix Coyotes hockey team. It was not complicated to reach Doan but my editor requested that I also interview Shane's wife, Andrea. The Doans have three small children and my interview was eventually set up at a nearby McDonald's. Admittedly it wasn't the ideal setting for an interview but I managed to gather the content for my story.

My interview with the Doans illustrates an experience I've had repeatedly when I interview someone. Because of the chaos during the interview, Shane and Andrea had no idea how I was going to piece together the story from the jumble of thoughts and stops and starts. Yet I had a clear-cut plan of attack for eventually writing the story.

Immediately following my interview, I took a few minutes to scratch down some outline points. I used these outline points to ultimately write the story and the sidebar with it. From my years of writing for various magazines and my years as a magazine editor, I suspected this story could be a cover story. While I hoped it would happen, I didn't write anything about it because I know often magazines shift those plans at the last minute. I was waiting until I saw the printed story.

During the interview (and toward the end of my story), Shane talked about his hopes to participate in the 2006 Winter Olympics in Turin, Italy. A Canadian, Doan was one of 35 NHL players selected to attend the Canadian Olympic Training Camp. "There are 700 NHL players and 67 percent of them are Canadian or 469 players," Doan explains. "It was an honor to be one of the 35 guys to possibly play on Team Canada." Shane had never been on this Olympic hockey team and at the time of our interview, he didn't know if he would be one of the 24 players ultimately selected to play in the Olympic Games. "If I get a chance to play on Team Canada, I will be there." After my interview, I learned Shane *was* selected to play for the team.

I've been able to meet some remarkable people through my interviews and you can have equal or even more amazing experiences in your writing life in the days ahead. It's a critical part of your writing life to understand the importance of interviews and the valuable information you can collect for your publishing and storytelling.

Dig Deeper

Writing books won't solve the stubborn celebrity profile or the impossible interview situation, but they can help refine your techniques. Each of these books contains helpful information.

1. *The Craft of Interviewing* by John Brady (Writer's Digest Books, 1977). This book contains a valuable mix between experiences of the author and step-by-step information on such areas as getting an interview, advance research, and formulating questions.

2. *Interviews That Work, A Practical Guide for Journalists* by Shirley Biagi (Wadsworth, Inc., 1992). This author has interviewed 46 expert interviewers such as Ted Koppel and Sam Donaldson on interview technique. The paperback covers the subject area with tips for the beginner and the expert.

3. *Before the Story, Interviewing and Communication Skills for Journalists* by George M. Killenberg and Rob Anderson (St. Martin's Press, 1989). This hardback is geared primarily to newspaper journalists but has an important emphasis on the relationship between the interviewer and the interviewee. It contains valuable information on meeting people and how to phrase your questions which can make or break an interview.

Awaken Your Dreams

1. Have you conducted many interviews? If you have, what new insights have you gained from this chapter that you can apply to your next interview?

2. If you haven't done many interviews, then make some specific plans to tackle some magazine work over the next month and decide who you will interview.

3. Do you have some dream interviews? I'm talking about personalities or celebrities that you would love to interview. Make a list of these people and then work toward accomplishing these dreams as you craft query letters to magazines and pitch story ideas. You will be amazed at the potential doors which will open because of your dreams and goals.

CHAPTER 9

Write for Print Magazines

You stare at a blank page. You roll the paper into the typewriter and sit there poised with your hands on the keys. Or maybe you turn on your computer and sit with an empty screen. What do you write?

Many writers and would-be writers have told me how that blank page petrifies them. In this chapter, we'll explore my technique for putting together a magazine article from idea to finished product.

Getting over the Hump

It's a rare day that I have trouble putting those initial words on paper. I always do some preparation ahead of time, and then use a slight trick. Ideas for magazine articles are everywhere and the places to write are just as plentiful. Maybe you have an interesting personal experience story you can capture? Possibly you have been involved in creating a new product that you'd like to share with readers through a how-to article.

Or if you don't have any material from your own experience to write about, consider interviewing interesting people around you and writing their story for publication.

The first question to ask is: Who is my audience? What publication will use this article? The possibilities are endless: adult, women, men, children, and teenagers. Are they in a specialized occupation such as schoolteachers? What age are they? The important thing is to be sure to target a specific audience and not make it for "everyone."

Every writer meets with rejection and develops projects which are never published. In fact, I have files of circulated but unpublished material. I caution you that rejection and unpublished articles are a part of the writer's life and the road to consistent publication.

Increase Your Odds to Get Published

The bulk of my magazine writing is done on assignment. How do you get an assignment? Through magazines you read on a consistent basis. Your familiarity with these publications and the types of articles that they publish gives you needed background.

As a first step, create a stack of the magazines that come into your home.

Organize them with several months from the same publication and then study the contents. What types of articles do they publish? How-to articles? Personal experience? For example, I used to be an editor at *Decision* magazine at the Billy Graham Evangelistic Association and almost every article was a first-person, personal experience story. If you study the magazine and notice this type of matter, then you submit a query or an article which is not written in the first person, you are asking for rejection. Or if you write a story about someone else in the third person, you will again invite rejection.

After you have studied the publications, then look online for their writer's guidelines. If you don't find them online, send an email or a simple letter asking for guidelines and enclose a self-addressed, stamped envelope for the response. You can find the address for the publication on the masthead of the magazine under editorial offices.

Reading through the guidelines gives you additional information. Does the publication accept query letters or prefer full manuscripts? Some magazines have a query only system. This means that you have to write a query letter and get a letter of request from the editor before sending the full manuscript. Other publications will accept a completed manuscript.

What's a query letter? While there are entire books written in answer to this question, I want to include a short overview. A query is a single-page letter that sells your story idea. It has a four paragraph formula. The first paragraph is simply to capture the editor's attention. I won't walk you through the day of an editor but because I've been one for years, I know they are involved in a multitude of tasks. Editors often read query letters at the end of the workday, in a carpool on the way home, or late at night. Your pitch must be interesting.

The second paragraph includes the basic outline or main points of how you will approach your subject. The third paragraph gives your personal qualifications for writing this article and your writing credits (if any). It basically answers the question, why should you of all the writers get this assignment? Highlight your area of expertise in this paragraph.

The final paragraph says how soon you can complete the article (give yourself enough time—for example, "three weeks from assignment") and says you are enclosing a self-addressed, stamped envelope or SASE and looking forward to their reply. I often send the letter to as many as ten different publications at the same time.

Within the magazine business, there is an ongoing discussion about simultaneous submissions (where you send the same original never-before–published finished article to several publications). If you do this, you may end up on the blacklist of authors. Each publication has a list of people that cannot write for the magazine and you don't want to be on that list. Also each publication has a list of authors they use regularly and call with ideas. Your goal is to join the regular contributors of the publication—particularly for those publications which pay promptly and pay well.

From my perspective, a simultaneous query is not the same as a finished article. Go ahead and query several magazines at the same time on the same topic if you think you can write several different articles on the same subject. One magazine may ask for 500 words on the topic, while another may approach it from an entirely different viewpoint and ask for 2,000 words. Your illustrations and information will be considerably different. If you send it to ten magazines, you may get ten rejections. On the other hand, perhaps you will get an acceptance or two, or at least a request to see the entire article on speculation. "On speculation" means that the editor is not under obligation to purchase your article if it doesn't meet the periodical's standards or expectations.

"IT'S FROM THE EDITOR. HE WANTS YOU TO SEND ANY FUTURE ANGRY LETTERS BY EMAIL."

A Word about Rejection

An article or query may be rejected for many reasons. Maybe the publication has recently published an article on that topic or they've assigned it to another author. Perhaps they have an article on that topic coming in an issue which is already in production but not printed. Reasons for rejection are often out of your control as a writer.

Sometimes even after a rejection, you can receive an assignment from a publication. Several years ago, I had queried a number of magazines about writing on listening to the audio version of the Bible. I targeted the January issues of publications for this short how-to article but every magazine rejected it.

Several weeks later, I received a phone call from a new editor at *Christian Life* magazine, one of the publications that had earlier rejected this idea. "We're sorting through some old queries," she explained. "Would you be able to write 500 words on the topic in the next three weeks?" I quickly agreed to the assignment and that little article turned into one of my most popular articles for reprint in other publications.

After You Decide on a Topic

Okay, you've decided on a publication and the type of article you are going to write. What next? You need to do research for the information you will use in the body of the article. I want to give you a word of caution about research. Make sure you have a specific ending to it. Some writers spend huge amounts of time in research and never sit down and write the article. How will you collect the information? Will it come from personal experience? Will you need stories from other people you need to interview? Will it involve library research for statistics? Make friends with the local librarians. They are a goldmine of information and resources.

You've gathered the research and raw information to pull together your magazine article. Now you are ready to begin writing. If you've written a query letter, then you already have the opening paragraph for your article. Otherwise, the first step in the writing process is to create a motivating opening story. The key phrase is to make it motivating. It has to propel the reader into the rest of the article so they can't stop reading.

Here's one example from my own personal story: "I've gone to church most of my life but I lived off my parent's faith until halfway through my sophomore year in college." How is that? Would it propel you to keep reading? It seems pretty boring to me and would not get me to read the article because the sentence tells the reader instead of involving the reader in the story. My published article for this personal story began, "I slapped the snooze alarm for the third time and finally opened my eyes at Chi Phi, my fraternity house. Last night had been a late one. After covering an evening speech and interview for the school paper, I worked frantically on the story until just before midnight, when I dropped it into the hands of a waiting editor."

Compare these two examples. Notice the detail in the second version. I am not telling you about the experience, I am showing you. Repeatedly the writing books and teachers say, "Show, don't tell." Many beginning writers don't understand this little slogan. Essentially it means that you need to include dialogue and the type of detail for a story which will interest the reader in the article.

After writing the opening, how do you continue? If you've done your research, you will not write 2,000 words for a publication that takes only 500 word articles. So you will have a target length for your article. This word count helps give definition to your plan.

Also if you've done your research, you've thought about the article and focused it. Can you summarize the point of the article into a single sentence? Complete the sentence: My article is about _____. After you've written this sentence, never wander away from this goal. As a magazine editor, I received articles that started out well then wandered around before the author reached a conclusion. These articles lacked focus. The sentence statement will help you keep the article on track.

I write from an outline. Normally my article will have a number of points or illustrations. A standard outline for an article would be: 1) describe the problem, 2) propose several possible solutions, and 3) finish with your solution. If you're writing about a person, your outline might include different aspects of the person's life. Write out the different points for your outline. When I write a short story, I use the same approach. Which parts will constitute the beginning, middle, and ending? An outline keeps you, the writer, focused on the goal of the article.

Also be realistic with yourself and your writing life. Can you write for only 30 minutes a day, or maybe only 10 minutes? Are you motivated to write the entire article in one session, or can you write only one point from your outline? Whatever your writing goal, I encourage you to write consistently and keep moving the article toward completion.

After you've written the article, put it away for a period of time. If you are on a tight deadline, that might involve eating lunch and then returning to it. If you have the time, you might be able to put it away for several days or a week. When you return to your article, I suggest you read it out loud because the ear is less forgiving than the eye. When you hear the words, it will be easier for you to spot areas in which you want to revise and rewrite.

Good Writing Is Rewriting

As you rework your article, here are some questions to consider: Does it make sense? Are there areas that are missing? Can you tell some of the stories with more detail and emotion? Is the article focused and targeted for the assigned publication? How about the ending? As a reader, how do you feel about it?

Try to look at your writing through objective and impersonal eyes. Consider the purpose of your article. Was it to motivate readers to action? Did it achieve its purpose?

Check the article for spelling and grammar mistakes. You'd be amazed to know how many articles are submitted for publication with typing errors and simple English errors. As a writer, you want to present the best article possible. Give it an additional check.

If you have the opportunity, allow a friend or fellow writer to read your article and give you feedback. I suggest that you use caution in this process of showing your article to someone else, however. Ultimately you are in charge of the contents of the article that you will submit. Don't soak up criticism like a sponge but carefully consider each comment. Does it have validity? If so, change it, and if not, ignore it.

The final step is to submit your material to a publication. In your cover letter to the editor, explain your familiarity with the magazine. If you've been taking it for years and faithfully reading it, say so. Don't exaggerate, but this familiarity shows your professional stance. Also, express your willingness to make any necessary changes. Maybe an editor will like your opening illustration but have a completely different direction for the article. If you've expressed willingness to revise, you will have an opportunity for publication. If you have the attitude, "I wrote it and this is it," then you'll miss that opportunity. The professional stance is to show flexibility.

A Final Word About Magazine Writing

There is no magic formula in writing for magazines. Instead, each article is written from a unique source which is you, the writer. While there is no formula, there is a standard format for your submission. Your manuscript needs to be submitted to the editor in a professional manner which means that it should be typed and double-spaced with generous margins. Some publications have specific guidelines for a particular section of the magazine in terms of the word length and essential elements. If you are writing one of these types of articles, you need to fulfill every requirement.

Each writer has to discover their place with words. The process of discovery takes initiative on your part to step out and try. It also involves getting some rejection but being persistent. Maybe you can't write teaching articles but you have a creative bent for teenagers. This process of self-discovery begins with a single step.

Several years ago, I received a letter from a prisoner who had read my biography about Romulo Saune called *One Bright Shining Path*. Other times, I have received letters from children who have enjoyed my books. We may never know the impact of our words and articles. As I read magazine articles and they motivate me to action and change, your articles can have the same impact.

Take the step and begin to fill that blank page or screen with words.

Dig Deeper

1. One of the basic magazine writing skills is to write a query letter and one of the best books in this area comes from Lisa Collier Cool called *How To Write Irresistible Query Letters* (Writer's Digest Books). This book gives step-by-step instructions on this critical area for magazine writing. Lisa is a contributing editor for a number of women's magazines and knows how to get great assignments through a one-page letter to the editor.

Awaken Your Dreams

1. Use the practical material in this article to plan several magazine articles that you will write over the next few months. Jot down specific goals for your writing. For example, decide to write three one-page query letters each week and send them to different magazines. If you consistently pitch editors, eventually you will land some assignments for your writing.

2. Make a goal that you will eventually write an article for a high paying publication. It may not happen immediately but it is good to have long-range goals for your magazine writing and continually make progress toward this goal.

CHAPTER 10

Participate in Writer's Organizations

"We can't say anything about it," my literary attorney and writer friend Sallie Randolph began. "But President Jimmy Carter and his wife Rosalynn are going to be at our member luncheon tomorrow."

I was in New York City for the annual conference of the American Society of Journalists and Authors (ASJA), the leading nonfiction writers group in the nation and originally known as the Society of Magazine Writers. Each year, the organization holds a large public conference on a Saturday in a hotel in New York City. Before this public conference, the ASJA has a much smaller member day meeting in the same location. One of our members had written a book with Rosalynn Carter and the authors were going to be given an award from the Society. The award winners were invited to attend the member luncheon and the Carters had accepted the invitation. There would be about 200 members and special guests at this luncheon.

While Sallie and I were not sitting at the table of honor with the former president and his wife, we figured out where the secret service would be sitting and were able to sit at that table. My business book, *Lessons from the Pit, A Successful Veteran of the Chicago Mercantile Exchange Shows Executives How to Thrive in a Competitive Environment* which I wrote for Joe Leininger, had just been released and I had a copy in my briefcase. During the meal, I asked the secret service agent when I could give President Carter a copy of my book. He said, "Do it right now because we're going to eat, speak, and leave."

With his permission, I walked over to the former president, introduced myself, and gave him a copy of my book which was published from B & H Publishing Group (formerly Broadman & Holman). I knew Broadman had been one of Jimmy Carter's publishers and he would be familiar with the company. He was gracious and thanked me.

As the meal concluded, the program began, the Carters spoke to the audience, and then quietly slipped out of the room—the president carrying one book out of that meeting—mine. I would not have been able to give him the book if I had not joined the ASJA. These unusual opportunities are one of the reasons to join a group and participate in their activities.

A conference in New York City is much more formal in attire than the typical writer's conference where the dress is casual. In New York City, I'm normally wearing a suit and matching pants. While I've been to many conferences, that ASJA conference where I met President Carter had one additional twist. When I arrived at my hotel, I noticed my bag was packed lighter than usual. I had left my hang up clothing in my closet at home and forgotten my suits. I called my wife who said, "Honey, you are in one of the largest cities in the world. Go buy yourself a new suit." The next morning I went into a men's store, purchased a suit and returned that afternoon for the adjusted pants. It is the only time in my travels that I've forgotten such a critical item and I was glad I had purchased a replacement since I had the opportunity at the members-only meeting to meet President Carter.

Get Away from Your Computer

Some people are joiners and others are not. I tend to fall into the joiner category and belong to a number of different organizations. As a writer and editor, I've learned a tremendous amount from these organizations, but I do more than simply learn. I take an active role of involvement—by choice.

Writing is a solitary action where you sit at your computer or typewriter and create words. While you may interview other people and do research, the actual writing is done alone. Yet there is a rich world of camaraderie for you as you participate in different writer's groups and organizations. From my personal experience, you will get much more out of an organization, if you volunteer and put something into it rather than simply attend the various programs.

About 20 years ago, I was on the staff of a magazine and one of my colleagues decided to start a writer's group in Orange County, California, where we lived. While my freelance writing was just beginning, Larry invited me to join the small board of directors for this group. As volunteers, we held Saturday meetings in the spring and the fall of each year. Before the conference we wrote to various magazines and book publishers asking for sample copies and writer's guidelines. The publishers and publications sent boxes of their samples to our meetings. One of my first activities in the group was to help set up these free samples (allowing us to gather our own copies before anyone came to the event). I was introduced to many magazines through these sample copies and guidelines.

There are hundreds of writing groups with different types of writers and focuses. As a writer, you can pay your dues and attend the event or you can volunteer and get more out of it. I recommend you become an active member of whatever group you join. The majority of these groups use volunteers for each aspect of the event—whether inviting the speakers or registering attendees at the door. What can you volunteer to do that will help the overall good of your group? Yes, it will take a bit of your time from writing, but from my perspective, it has been time well-spent.

During those early days at the Orange County Christian Writers Group, I met several key editors who are still active in publishing today. My relationship with these editors and literary agents began through a writer's organization.

The Power of the Group

I'm convinced that in certain situations, a group has more power and can accomplish more than any single individual. There are many reasons to join groups, but my greatest learning has come from my active involvement. For example, I serve on several ASJA committees and work behind the scenes as a volunteer. A number of years ago, I served on the board of the Evangelical Press Association and formed long-lasting relationships with numerous editors. Some of those editors have gone into book publishing while others remain in the magazine area.

Maybe you've seen the bumper sticker proclaiming, "Writers do it alone." It is true that writing is a solitary craft. You take a legal pad or a keyboard somewhere and write words for other people to read. In many ways, I'm a quiet person and in other ways I love organizations. I've found incredible value in absorbing information from others in a group setting. Also I know that the information and collective effort of a group can literally cut years of struggle from the individual writer as I will later explain.

There are many large and small writers' organizations. In the next few pages, I will highlight some excellent large organizations and stress the benefits for the person who joins. Some of these organizations have membership requirements you might not be able to meet during the early portion of your writing career. Even if you don't meet these requirements for membership, however, it is valuable for you to attend their public conferences and have the goal of one day joining.

Writer's Organizations

American Society of Journalists and Authors (ASJA)

Founded in 1948, the American Society of Journalists and Authors is the nation's leading organization of independent nonfiction writers. The ASJA membership consists of more than 1,300 outstanding freelance writers of magazine articles, trade books, and other forms of nonfiction writing, each of whom has met ASJA's exacting standards of professional achievement. As a member of the ASJA for several years, I've found the organization to be excellent and provides great resources for the new writer (through the public pages) and the professional writer (through the member-only section). Their annual conference is one of the best in the U.S.

The Authors Guild

The Authors Guild is the nation's oldest and largest professional society of published authors, representing more than 8,000 writers. The Guild and its parent organization, the Authors League of America, have achieved much for individual authors through the collective power and voice of their members—from improvement of contracts and royalty statements, to protection of authors' rights under the First Amendment, to the redress of damaging tax inequities.

The Guild's legal staff reviews its members' publishing and agency contracts, intervenes in publishing disputes, and holds seminars and symposia on issues of importance to writers. The Guild also lobbies on the national and local levels on behalf of all authors on issues such as copyright, taxation, and freedom of expression. Reports to members bring them up-to-date on professional issues of immediate importance, and give them the information necessary to negotiate from a position of strength. The membership requirements for The Authors Guild are less strict than the ASJA. I've enjoyed their newsletter and my limited involvement in this organization.

The Society of Children's Book Writers & Illustrators

The Society of Children's Book Writers and Illustrators, formed in 1971 by a group of Los Angeles-based writers for children, is the only international organization to offer a variety of services to people who write, illustrate, or share a vital interest in children's literature. The SCBWI acts as a network for the exchange of knowledge between writers, illustrators, editors, publishers, agents, librarians, educators, book sellers, and others involved with literature for young people. There are currently more than 19,000 members worldwide, in over 70 regions, making it the largest children's writing organization in the world. While I am not currently a member of this organization, I have been previously, particularly when I was writing children's books. Their network in the children's book area is unparalleled above any other group.

Evangelical Press Association

The Evangelical Press Association embraces some 375 periodicals, organizations, and individual members. Its 250-plus periodical members have a combined circulation of more than twenty million readers. EPA is a religious and educational nonprofit corporation under the laws of the state of California, managed by an executive director, who is responsible to a board of six directors. As a magazine editor, I've been a part of this organization and attended their annual conferences for many years. Because I'm not currently with a member magazine staff, I'm an "associate member." I find the association valuable and it is a great group of writers and editors.

For Fiction Writers

If you write fiction, then three organizations you might consider joining are Romance Writers of America, The American Christian Fiction Writers, and the Mystery Writers of America. Each of these organizations have specific membership requirements and writers benefit from joining their ranks.

Other Lists of Writer's Organizations

If these organizations aren't right for you, then I suggest you look at these locations:

- www.readersread.com/organizations.htm

- www.dmoz.org/Arts/Writers_Resources/Organizations

- www.forwriters.com/groups.html

If you have not found an organization for your writing, then use Google and do a bit of searching until you find the right one for you. It may take some experimentation, but the experience of these new friends and the knowledge you gain from these organizations will take years off the learning curve of getting published. You instantly connect with like-minded people who are writing similar material. I like the little slogan tossed about within the American Society of Journalists and Authors: "We train our competition." It is true.

Dig Deeper

1. Use the *Writer's Market* or other resources mentioned in this chapter to learn about various groups. Are there some in your local area? Are there national organizations that you would like to participate in and learn from?

2. Select several of these groups that involve your particular interest as a writer and join these groups.

Awaken Your Dreams

1. Choose to take an active role in at least one writer's organization. Be aware that volunteering will take time away from your writing but your participation has other benefits.

2. Can you write for the organization newsletter? Many of these organizations have internal publications. Writing for these newsletters will be good experience, plus you will raise your own visibility within the organization. These new relationships could be exactly what you need to take your writing to the next level and help you achieve your writing dreams.

CHAPTER 11

Build Your Platform

"Focus, focus, focus," one of my friends said when I told her about the diverse efforts in my writing life. And she's right in that to complete anything successfully—and especially something the length of a book project—you will need to have a consistent focus on the project for days on end.

Yet there is a danger with a single focus for your writing. I've met many writers who have focused only on a lengthy fiction project and never considered writing anything smaller such as a short story or a nonfiction magazine article. Because of their single-minded focus, they have never experimented with other writing forms to their own detriment, thereby failing one of the key ingredients for any successful writer and not building a body of work.

When someone looks into the volume of writing that I've done over the years, they often approach me wide-eyed and ask, "How in the world did you do it?" Yes, I've written for more than 50 printed magazines and published more than 60 books with traditional publishers—and my first book was released in 1992. I compare all of that writing to the way you eat an elephant. You do it one bite at a time and you write the words one page at a time.

Almost 20 years ago, I was on the faculty of an East Coast writer's conference because of my role as a magazine editor. After landing at the airport, I had a couple hours of riding in a van to reach this facility and I sat in the back with one other faculty member—a literary agent. I had never met this person and we spent the time getting acquainted and talking about long-term goals for our publishing dreams.

During our conversation, this agent pointed out something that has become somewhat of a mantra for my own writing life. He said, "Every writer needs to build a body of work and just look at Jerry B. Jenkins." Both of us knew Jerry personally, the author of the best-selling Left Behind series. At that time, I believe Jerry had written 60 or 70 books, but his fiction writing was just getting started. His specialty at that time was writing books for well-known people like Meadowlark Lemon from the Harlem Globetrotters or the evangelist Luis Palau. We marveled at the volume of writing which Jerry had in print—and it's much greater today.

"Jerry didn't just wake up one day and decide to write 60 books," the agent explained. "For years, he has been actively building a body of work."

It was a lesson I've never forgotten and has driven the diversity of my own writing life. While I've written longer projects like books, I've also focused on writing shorter magazine articles and online Ebooks and many other types of writing. Each type of writing builds that body of work.

Throughout the publishing world—whether magazine or book or online—your experience weighs into the consideration process with the editor. The buzz or consistent phrase says, "Writers need to build a platform." Whether you write nonfiction or fiction, the platform (which is another way of saying your visibility in the marketplace) is important because that's how you attract—and keep—readers.

What are you doing today to build your platform or your body of work? Are you balanced in your approach to your writing or have you fallen into the danger of a single focus without looking at the big picture?

When a writer wants to write a book, they will ask at what point do they begin their marketing efforts. In traditional publishing, books often take months to get through the system before they are published. While there is no universal starting point for your marketing efforts, it is hard to begin too soon.

In Steve Weber's *Plug Your Book!* (www.snipurl.com/plugbk), he includes a relevant quote from best-selling author Seth Godin who says, "The best time to start promoting your book is three years before it comes out. Three years to build a reputation, build a permission asset, build a blog, build a following, build credibility, and build the connections you'll need later."

It doesn't take much for me to imagine all of the authors who moan, "Three years!" As the author, you have the greatest vision and passion for your book—no matter how you publish it. The publisher's attention will be divided with other titles and matters, where you can steadily focus on your book. Potential readers need continual reminders about the availability of your book and why it is relevant to their needs. In the case of my *Book Proposals That Sell*, I've seen a steady increase in the sales of this book since it was released several years ago. At first, the more experienced writers would tell me that they knew how to write a book proposal and had read other books on the topic so they didn't purchase my book until later. When they finally got around to reading it, they appreciated my unique perspective and the valuable information it contained—even if they had read other books.

If you are looking for the end point to your marketing efforts for a book, again as the author you will have the greatest passion for your book. If your book goes out of print and your passion for the book has failed, then you can stop marketing it. Otherwise I would encourage you to continue your efforts—even if it is only once a week or once a month. You never know which one of your efforts will be the tipping point to move your sales rapidly ahead.

Is Giving Away Content Valuable?

It is completely counterintuitive to give away valuable content. Often new or unpublished writers will ask whether they will lose their rights or be hurt if they give away their written material online.

While I understand their fears of their idea being stolen, from my personal experience of many years in publishing, I have never seen it happen. Yes, I've seen people pitch similar ideas but I've never had one of my exact ideas stolen from either my work online or my printed writing. I've actually been too busy writing and producing new material to spend a lot of time worrying about it. In many ways, it's the complete wrong focus for a would-be writer.

Instead, I'd encourage them to be focused on learning the craft of storytelling and how to shape their words into compelling prose. It's a better use of their time and energy. Whether you have written nonfiction or fiction, if you have written something valuable, you can give that information away—and attract readers. For example, I'm giving away my *Straight Talk from the Editor* Ebook (www.straighttalkeditor.com) in exchange for you giving me your first name and email address. I'm also giving away a 90-page Ebook about book proposal creation with the same exchange at www.bookproposalcoach.com.

Maybe you've written an excellent novel and are trying to figure out how to get attention for it. Could you achieve that attention through giving it away?

Book marketing expert John Kremer[17] tells the story of a Brazilian author who for years has been an apostle of free Internet distribution.

> In 1999, best-selling author Paulo Coelho, who wrote *The Alchemist*, was failing in Russia. That year he sold only about 1,000 books, and his Russian publisher dropped him. But after he found another, Coelho took a radical step. On his own Web site, launched in 1996, he posted a digital Russian copy of *The Alchemist*.
>
> With no additional promotion, print sales picked up immediately. Within a year he sold 10,000 copies; the next year around 100,000. By 2002 he was selling a total of a million copies of multiple titles. Today, Coelho's sales in Russian are over 10 million and growing. "I'm convinced it was putting it up for free on the Internet that made the difference," he said in an interview at the World Economic Forum in Davos.
>
> Coelho explained why he thinks giving books away online leads to selling more copies in print: "It's very difficult to read a book on your computer. People start printing out their own copies. But if they like the book, after reading 30-40 pages they just go out and buy it." By last year Coelho's total print sales worldwide surpassed 100 million books.

"Publishing is in a kind of Jurassic age," Coelho continues. "Publishers see free downloads as threatening the sales of the book. But this should make them rethink their entire business model." Now Coelho is a convert to the Internet way of doing things. His online e-mail newsletter, published since 2000, has 200,000 subscribers.

While this story about Coelho is a great success story in the publishing world, make sure you see one of the keys—brilliant storytelling is foundational. You must understand the needs of the audience or market, meet that need with excellent writing. All too often, I've seen people attempt to give away material which does not fall into this excellent category and does little to help them in their audience building intent. There is a delicate balance between learning marketing skills and learning the craft of writing.

Visibility Is Key

Repeatedly writers tell me about this experience so I know it is a common one. Writers have a dream to get published so they write a book (fiction or nonfiction), then pitch it to me at a writer's conference or through an email query or a printed pitch that comes in the mail. Yet when you look at the section "about the author" you find they have little visibility in the public eye and, if pressed, they would confess to being "unknown." They may speak (every now and then) or write a magazine article (every now and then). They have disconnected from a key factor of visibility—or one of the keys to selling books in the marketplace and to a publisher. Yes, it is about the craft of telling a good story or shaping a good idea with a need in the market. If you have ten or 100 great stories in your office as an editor or literary agent, which ones are you going to champion? It's the ones from the author who has built an audience.

Some of the writers who dislike this topic are fiction writers. In fact, some of them freely admit they are writing fiction because they don't have to have a platform or visibility. It's true, to write fiction, the storytelling is key but it is also important to have visibility in the marketplace and connect to an audience who loves your writing. That acquired audience is what drives readers to the bookstore when their favorite author has released another novel.

In this instant world, many authors shrug when I encourage them to carve out their specialty and build that audience in the marketplace.

"Too much work," some of them think.

"I don't know where to begin," others complain.

If you are looking for some insight about where to begin or some more ideas for visibility, I recommend Steven Van Yoder's *Get Slightly Famous*. The book is not specifically targeted to writers but every author can gain ideas from it.

If you are overwhelmed with the competition in your area of the marketplace, how do you stand out and shine? Van Yoder provides a cornucopia of ideas to move anyone from an unknown position to becoming a slightly famous standout. He defines "slightly famous" as "Just famous enough to make their names come to mind when people are looking for a particular product or service, and let them reap the benefits. They get more business—not only more, but the right kind of business—and they don't have to work so hard to get it."[18]

While the marketplace may seem crowded (pick your market), there is always room for innovative communicators who will gain visibility and credibility and become thought leaders. Through dozens of case studies and stories, Van Yoder proves his points. The first section helps the reader think through their own distinctive style, the second portion explores different media strategies (for different types of media such as print, online, broadcast), and the final section gives a wealth of ideas for anyone to expand their own reach.

The book is well-written, easy to use, and one that I'm certain you will use your highlighter in and go back to review the concepts and apply them to your own business.

Imitate Good Ideas

I am constantly looking for good ideas that I can imitate and apply to my own writing life and publishing work. I hope you will apply these marketing concepts to your own dreams of getting published and building a platform.

If you want to write a memoir or personal story, I'd encourage you to look closely at this interview where Alex Mandossian interviewed Julie Andrews. You can listen to the interview now in replay (www. terrylinks.com/JA). While the book is a memoir, notice what they are giving away to people who come to this book tour Web site. It's not a portion of the book but a series of tips about how to get the most out of reading with your child. Yes, the site pushes people toward the memoir but Julie Andrews and her daughter, Emma Walton Hamilton, also have a series of children's books. I found this sort of cross-marketing effort fascinating. If you are pitching or writing a memoir, you can imitate this good idea for your project.

If You Have a Book to Promote

One of the most effective ways to sell books is through public speaking and holding personal events. These events can be large or small. Some of these events are teleseminars and do not involve any travel. They only involve speaking to an audience on the telephone.

Other events like a conference or a seminar involve traveling and speaking in person. I encourage you to have a "speaking" section on your website. I have a place on my personal site where I continually update my forthcoming speaking at http://terrylinks.com/sked. Also I regularly promote these events through social media such as Twitter and Facebook plus through my regular newsletters. Take a few minutes and use this idea for your own writing work. You never know how it will pay off for you.

**"Do you have any kind of E-Newsletter
that'll keep me up with events in the jungle?"**

More on Building a Platform

Whether it is in the queries or book proposals that come across my acquisitions editor work, or the questions I am asked at a writer's conference or in any other setting, most writers seem to understand publishers are looking for authors with platforms. I want to be clear because publishers do not build platforms but look for authors who already have built their own platform. This situation has been true in nonfiction for some time but it is also important for fiction authors.

Many writers groan when they hear this news. They feel rejected and slink off somewhere to moan to each other. In my view, they need to stop such actions and begin to build their platforms. Yes, it will take time. It takes time to learn your writing craft and marketing skills and many other things. Start a newsletter and then regularly build your audience. Here is a 150-page FREE Ebook resource: www.terrylinks. com/E101. Get this book, print it out, and study it, then start your own newsletter and audience building for your own platform.

As a model in this area of building a platform, I suggest you watch *New York Times* best-selling author Debbie Macomber (www. debbiemacomber.com). Several years ago I was at a conference with Debbie and she orchestrated a mob scene for her book signing at the local Barnes and Nobles in Amarillo, Texas. Several years ago, a Seattle newspaper interview mentioned that Debbie had over 70,000 names on her list. An article in a later issue of *Publishers Weekly* showed that Debbie continues to grow this list of readers and it is now over 100,000 strong. Her fellow novelists were amazed at how Debbie is using this list. First, she has grown this list over 25 years in the business and second, she uses the data to tell people about her book signings in a particular area of the country which attracts new readers. I believe it's another good idea that any author can do. It will not happen overnight but you can begin today to take some steps in this direction for your writing life.

Some of these practices are easy but will take time and investment. Are you willing to chisel away at it and make it happen? I'm encouraging you to take action and use the good ideas that come across your path.

Don't Forget These Book Facts

Once a year, Bowker, the leading provider of bibliographic information in North America, releases statistics concerning the book publishing industry and its production numbers for the previous year. The number of books produced in 2011 broke another record at 347,178 new titles, or an increase of 6 percent from the previous year.

You can read the full release and see some other book numbers (www.terrylinks.com/USbk2011).

From these production numbers, we learn that it's never been easier to get a book published. The proliferation of self-publishing, new publishers, and Print On Demand (POD) publishers make it possible for anyone to get a printed book. You can write a manuscript, take it down to one of these places, and have a bound book for your shelf or to give to your relatives.

One of the hardest things to proofread is something which doesn't appear on the page. What isn't said in these production numbers? These facts don't say anything about books sold or books read or (even rarer) books which make the best-seller list.

I don't know about you, but I'm not interested in writing books that aren't read and aren't sold. Certainly I can crank a bunch of words into the computer and go to a self-publishing place and get it bound into a book. If I have no means to sell it, then I only contribute to the paper proliferation rather than raising the number of people who are reading. As a July 12, 2004 *Publisher's Weekly* article pointed out, "A survey conducted by the National Endowment for the Arts has confirmed a trend that most book publishing industry members are well aware of: the percentage of Americans who read books has steadily declined over the last 20 years." Yes, traditional publishing takes time and energy and patience. The marketing effort for a book takes a lot of energy and effort. But if it is read, then it's worth the effort to build your platform.

Dig Deeper

1. To learn more about how to create a platform, I recommend you read Stephanie Chandler's *The Author's Guide to Building an Online Platform, Leveraging the Internet to Sell More Books* (Quill Diver Books, 2008). My five-star review of this book on Amazon says,

   > Every writer has great dreams and aspirations of selling many copies of their published book. Stephanie Chandler gives you the real story about publishers. They can make beautiful well-crafted books but what about selling those books? That's a key responsibility for the author. *The Author's Guide to Building an Online Platform* gives writers the critical tools to sell their books into the marketplace. As Chandler writes at the bottom of the first page of chapter 1, "The reality in the world of publishing is that without marketing, a book simply cannot be successful. And even if you have the biggest publishers on the planet behind you, it is unlikely that they will run your entire marketing campaign for you. You will still be required to do the majority of the work. Publishers use the word "platform" a great deal and Chandler explains, "The formation of a platform is essential for publishing nonfiction and helpful for writers of fiction. A platform encompasses your ability to reach a broad audience before the book is even released.... Authors of fiction and gift books aren't always required to have a platform first. But if you come to the table with one, your chances of getting published will be dramatically increased. Agents and publishers want authors who can sell books. Once you realize that and figure out how to demonstrate that you can do that your future in publishing will be bright" (page 6). In a no-nonsense style, Chandler

gives you the details to stand apart from the run-of-the-mill book submission or published book author—because you will be motivated and informed to sell more books.

2. The second book I recommend as an additional resource is Steven Van Yoder's *Get Slightly Famous* (Bay Tree Publishing, 2007). Every writer can learn important strategies for attracting consistent media attention and learn how to use speaking engagements to cultivate their target market.

Awaken Your Dreams

1. Plan some concrete steps to begin to build your platform.

2. First identify your target audience and then start an online newsletter or use other ideas from this chapter to begin connecting with your readers. It will take time but while you are learning the craft of writing, you can also be building an audience for your writing.

CHAPTER 12

Continue to Train

As a writer, I was sure my story idea held fascination—yet I could not find any magazine to publish it. I had worked carefully on my query letter and had sent it out to the major magazines in the category of the article. All I received in response for my efforts were form rejections. With the arrival of each response, my frustration increased. I was certain the story had an audience and my only question was where could I find a publication to print it?

I thought maybe I wasn't looking at it from the right perspective. Perhaps I needed help and insight beyond my own resources. So I took the story to my local critique group. They thought my writing was good and they liked the story. Why couldn't I get a magazine editor to like it?

Then I decided to send it to multiple magazines at the same time so I could get varied responses from the editors. Sometimes a publication will want only 1,000 words while other times they will want only

500 words on the topic—no matter the length you've proposed in your query letter.

At the time, I was writing many articles for the magazines I was pitching. I was a known writer, yet the only response from my pitches was these printed letters which essentially said, "Thank you but no thank you." I had no information or insight about the real reasons behind the rejection and with each response my frustration increased.

I was pitching the story of a transformed life. A former pastor had two fronts to his marriage relationship—one that showed in public which was kind and gentle, then another one in private which was locked into consistent verbal combat with his wife. This couple would be verbally sparring on the way to church on Sunday morning, and then arrive and he would deliver a dynamic message to his large congregation.

One night he insisted on climbing onto his roof in the rain to fix his television antenna. It doesn't take much common sense to see the foolishness of such a decision. He fell off the roof and hit his head on the concrete patio. In the hospital the doctors told him that he would never walk again. This pastor pleaded with God that if He would heal him, he would spend the rest of his life loving his wife and changing his behavior. God responded and while medically it could not be explained, the pastor's health was restored and he did indeed change his life. Together, with his wife, they formed a marriage ministry which has transformed thousands of couples.

I called my story, "Shocked into Service" and searched for a magazine to publish it yet I was getting repeatedly rejected with no explanation.

That spring I attended a writer's conference and signed up for a brief meeting with one editor who had rejected my pitch. My agenda during the meeting was simple: I wanted to understand the reason I could not find a publication for my story.

During my meeting with the editor, I asked for honest feedback and the editor leveled with me. At that time, the PTL scandal with Jim and Tammy Faye Bakker had dominated the stories in the news.

"People do not want to know their pastor fights with his wife, and then arrives at the church like nothing is wrong and delivers their sermon," he explained. "While the changes in his life are admirable, this duality in his life is keeping your story from getting published."

With this editor's insight, my frustration was erased and I understood why my idea had been rejected. If I had not met with this long-time editor and asked for his specific feedback, I would have never understood the reasons.

In reality, editors and literary agents do not normally give such specific feedback when they reject writer's ideas, queries and submissions. That is not their role. Instead they are tasked to see if the idea is a fit for their publication or publishing house—a yes or a no decision. They don't critique the idea or give detailed feedback. Yes, there are critique services where you can pay for such feedback but one of the best places to get it is in a one-on-one session with an experienced professional at a writer's conference.

There are many reasons to attend a writer's conference. Your attendance can cut years off the learning curve to getting published. It's a personal investment. Whether you attend for a full day or spend several days, it will involve investing your time, energy, and money. In this chapter, I will explore some of the reasons to attend these meetings and provide information on where to find these gatherings.

Like many other kinds of businesses, the writing business is relational. Talent, craft and skill does enter the consideration but it's also *who you know.* Possibly you are new to this field and you are saying, "I don't know *anyone.*" That's OK. Everyone has to begin somewhere in this journey, but you don't have to stay in that situation. Through writer's conferences, you can begin to form editor relationships.

Almost 20 years ago, I began attending conferences. I worked on a magazine staff that understood the benefits and, accordingly, we used our slim financial resources to send our employees. It helped their professional development and also helped improve their ability to work on our magazine. I've also attended conferences simply for my own personal development and professionalism.

In recent years, I've represented publishing houses as an acquisitions editor and a literary agent at these gatherings. For several years I was a literary agent. As an editor and an agent, the experience has been eye-opening to me and changed some of my perspectives. I have some amazing stories about pushy conferees trying to convince me to purchase a particular manuscript. This usually backfires and makes the editor or agent want to run instead of listen carefully to your idea. Always remember that you want to make a good impression on the editor or the agent, not a negative one.

As an acquisitions editor, I continue to attend at least one conference a year as a regular conferee—i.e. a paying participant and not someone who represents a publisher or magazine or goes to teach workshops. One conference I regularly attend for my own development is the annual conference for the American Society of Journalists and Authors in New York City. At this conference I've met editors from *Ladies Home Journal, Woman's Day, Modern Maturity, Money* magazine, and book editors from publishers such as Random House, Simon and Schuster, and Penguin.

Conferences have been a large part of my writing career. Often at these conferences, editors and agents are inundated with the wrong material because writers haven't done their homework. They may send inappropriate material to the wrong place and waste everyone's time—the writer, the editor, and the agent. At a writer's conference, you meet the editors face-to-face and realize they are real people. This process begins to form your relationship. Then when you send in your material, they recall your name, or you can bring it to their attention saying, "It was great to meet you at _____ conference."

Three Pieces of Advice

1. Do your homework. Know who will be attending the conference and read in advance what a particular editor needs and acquires (the *Writer's Market* is a good place to start). Then craft an idea, a proposal, or something to start the conversation with the editor. Give them something they need. Editors read lots of stuff that they don't need at these conferences. They are looking for the jewel in the stack. It could be *your* writing if you do your homework.

2. Make a point to get to know different editors—even outside of your particular genre. What you write this year may change next year. Even if you've never written a book, get to know the book editors. Sit at their tables and talk with them about your hopes and dreams. And throughout the week, make note of things you want to remember—then read your notes when you get home and follow through. You would be surprised how few people actually execute the necessary follow-through work.

3. Learn your craft but also look to expand your writing horizon. This advice is for newcomers but also for the veteran. I'd encourage everyone to take a class outside of what they normally take. If you don't write for children, take a children's workshop. If you have never written a personal experience article, take a

one-hour workshop on this topic. It could open a new door of opportunity in your writing life.

I've made some dear friends at writer's conferences and that's why I look forward to returning. It's my opportunity to help others and give back. I'm constantly learning new things as a writer—and a writer's conference is the perfect place to learn.

From my perspective, writer's conferences have been life-changing events and have been critical in my professional and personal development. I recommend you take the time, energy, and resources to attend one.

Plan for Success

Don't you feel the urge to rush, rush, and then rush a bit more? I believe such an attitude is inherent in our get-it-done-quick world. We know we need to attend a writer's conference for our own encouragement and to form new relationships with editors. We save our money and make a commitment to attend, yet we fail to put energy into our preparation. What editors do we want to meet? What pitch will we give those editors? If we fail to do this advance work, we won't get the maximum benefit from our attendance.

Notice I wrote that last paragraph in the plural tense as I include myself in this category. Almost every year, I plan a trip to New York City and attend the annual conference of the American Society of Journalists and Authors (ASJA) Conference in April or May. When I register for the conference, they request tentative decisions about the different workshops that I will be attending so they can plan the size of the rooms. While it is wise to select these workshops as a good first step, it is much harder to study the specific editors, research their publication, and plan some appropriate pitches.

This type of planning will increase the effectiveness of your queries to the editors. At the ASJA meetings, they have added sessions called personal pitch. Book editors, magazine editors, and literary agents agree to meet with ASJA members or professional writers for a specific period of time. These pitch sessions are like speed dating for editors because they are ten minutes each and the time frames are strictly maintained. There is little time to flounder or ask general questions of the editor if you want to get an assignment. Instead, you have to think about the publication, plan out several provocative (and appropriate) article ideas, and then rapidly fire them to the editor. These brief sessions are enough to exchange business cards and receive a reaction from the editor. While it feels great to receive a positive reaction to your oral pitch, the key to a real assignment and getting published will be in the follow-through. Whether it is magazine or book publishing, it is not decided on an oral pitch. The key will be your actual writing. Whether in person or on the telephone, someone's idea may sound terrific but the real grabber is how it works in print. I encourage you to follow up on your ideas after the conference. You would be surprised at the writers who never do this after a positive oral pitch.

Essential for Every Conference

One other tool—which faculty members and participants often fail to have—is a simple business card with contact information including your name, address, email, phone number, and Web site to exchange with an editor or another writer. If you don't have a card, there is nothing to exchange—and it's harder to get those valuable business cards and contact information from the editor. Those cards can be the beginnings of a terrific relationship. I also recommend using uncoated paper for the back of your cards so the recipient can write on the back of it. When you receive a card, I recommend jotting down something on the back that reminds you of that particular person as you will collect many cards at a single event.

Writers have asked whether they should take a laptop computer to the conference. My answer depends on the conference and whether you will make time in your schedule to use it. Sometimes I've found hauling my laptop to a conference a complete waste of time. There hasn't been any outside phone line or anything wireless or any means to read my email. Often the conference centers are in remote locations and there are no telephones in the room. It's an intentional part of the setting to get you away from the phone and television, but it makes it difficult to keep up on your email.

On the other hand, several times a computer has been vital during a conference. Several years ago during an event, I faced a stiff book deadline so every spare minute I was back in my room cranking out more pages for my project. In this case, my book deadline took priority over my leisure time at the conference and made that particular conference less enjoyable to me. You have to think carefully about how much you will use your laptop and if using it will take away from other things you could take advantage of during the conference. I find some of the most productive moments of a conference often occur while I am sitting around talking with people. Whether you take your laptop to a writer's conference or not is an individual choice.

The first preparation for a conference is with your own attitude and heart. Be prepared to listen to the editor. Their input may take your article or book idea in a different direction and you have to be open to that sort of input instead of being firmly fixed on your own idea. The editor knows what's best for their particular publishing house. They hold the keys to publication and we need to listen to them.

Also be prepared for rejection. In this business, we get rejected a lot—I certainly do and it's never easy. One way to handle rejection is to write more and get more things into the mail. Maybe your particular idea wasn't the right one for that editor and it will be right somewhere else. Or maybe in the big picture you were to write that article or proposal or book as a part of your training for something else. I've got plenty of things in my files which have never been published, and I know many other writers could say the same.

When you talk with editors, understand that their rejection is not personal. Every editor has their own viewpoint. The publishing world is very subjective. One person loves it and another doesn't. Realize that each editor has their own individual needs. Your article might be perfect in another magazine. At the same time, be prepared to hear an honest comment from the editor's perspective. If it resonates right with your spirit, then take the comment and make the revision.

Also prepare to take a learner's stance in your session with the editor. If they don't need your article or book, what do they need? Take notes and then find out how you can fulfill this need. When I met with one editor, she liked my idea but expressed a greater interest in a completely different project. I wrote down her idea and on the way home, I created several new ideas which were more on target with her need. You can take the same approach with other editors. Their needs will not necessarily be your first idea, yet be something you "could" write for them.

Finally when you meet with an editor, be prepared to build a relationship. The publishing community is a small world. A wise editor is on the lookout for writers whom he or she can turn to again and again for their publication or publishing house. You are building a relationship which could continue for years. At one large conference, I spent a few minutes talking with the president of a large publishing house. He was rushing off to an appointment but stopped for a minute to talk with me. While I have known this leader for 15 years, I mentioned that I had never written a book for their publishing house. I had sent in proposals but it was not the right idea at the right time. When he encouraged me to send him ideas, I reversed the question and said, "Hey, you've got ideas. Send me some of those ideas." We both laughed but he recognized the truth in my request. Magazine editors and book publishers have ideas and books they create and want to publish. Because I asked for his ideas, maybe he will unexpectedly call me with an assignment. Develop your relationships at these training events. You never know when they will lead to another opportunity.

Dig Deeper

1. Use a *Writer's Market* or search using Google to find a conference in your interest area and plan to attend at least one of these events each year.

2. One of the best writers' conferences is held twice a year and called Author 101 University (www. author101-university.com). Rick Frishman, publisher at Morgan James, brings together agents and editors from many different areas of the publishing community to focus on different ways to market and sell books. You will find this event can be life-changing and is highly recommended.

Awaken Your Dreams

1. Take advantage of a resource like Epic Print Solutions (www.epicprintsolutions.com) to produce your business cards and give them to faculty members and writers at the event.

2. Take active steps before the conference to prepare, during the conference to capture ideas and pitches that receive a positive response, then after the conference follow up on these pitches.

3. If you can't make it to a conference right away, then explore alternative methods such as teleseminars and learning online. Begin at: www.askterrywhalin.com or www.asksusandriscoll.com or www.askandymcguire.com. Each of these three teleseminars has already been held and is on "replay mode." Instead of asking a question, put "no question" and reach the page where you can instantly download the teleseminar to your computer or iPod.

CHAPTER 13

Create a Presence Online

One of my writer friends does not have a Web site or a blog or any presence online. I've talked with her several times and encouraged her to start something but she's not interested. If you Google her name, you will learn in the first entry that she has written over 90 books with over three million books in print, among other things. Yes, her publishers display her books online but you will be challenged to find anything personal about this author.

Times Have Changed

Several years ago, it was okay for an author not to have a Web site. In fact, there was a great deal of skepticism about anything online and whether it was true or not. There were many examples of people who built complete false identities online through Web sites that stretched the truth. The pendulum has now swung the other direction, however. While it's a good idea to have some degree of skepticism about the information you find online, in today's publishing climate, the Internet is often the first place people turn for information about anything and anyone.

As literary agent Richard Curtis explains, "When I pitch authors to editors over the phone, I can actually hear them typing on the keyboard as we speak. I know that while we're talking, they are going on Google or Amazon and checking out the author. They'll say, 'I see, oh yeah, I see the author's picture or the cover of his last five books.'"

What do they find when they Google your name?

Open a window in your Internet browser and go to Google.com. Type your own name into the search window and see what you find. From time to time, it's a good habit for anyone in publishing to check this information. This exercise will give you some idea of your level of presence online.

At a recent writer's conference, I heard Rick Frishman, Publisher at Morgan James Publishing, tell the audience about the importance of every would-be author knowing their own reputation online. He described a situation where a major book was cancelled over something an editorial assistant found about the author on the 25th or 26th page of Google. You may not think that a publisher will go to that level of vetting for an author. Be aware some publishers will invest this level of checking your public information online as when you become one of their authors their reputation is hooked to your background.

Because of the ease of accessibility and many other factors, every writer needs to have visibility on the Internet.

"Looks like Eric's ready to go fulltime with his online business."

Ways to Begin Your Web Presence

I remember my fears when I wanted to launch my first Web site several years ago. I didn't know the first thing about where to go and what to do.

So I took the most logical step and asked around within my network of friends and acquaintances and found someone to help me. A web designer in another part of the country was happy to work with me. I looked at her work and liked what I saw, and then we negotiated a reasonable price and a schedule of production deadlines.

I worked intensively on that first Web site, what it said about my writing and my work, the articles it displayed, along with a bookstore section for my various books in print. We had several weeks of intense back and forth email conversations. I constantly checked the Web site and its development and finally everything was in place. I had a well-designed, practical Web site which was essentially a static brochure about my writing work.

After several weeks, I wanted to change something. No problem. The designer changed it. Then I received the bills for these minor changes—and that's when I developed a strong desire to learn everything I could learn about web design and some basic HTML skills.

As you launch your Web site, you have to make a basic choice whether you are going to have someone else do it (outsource is the big buzz word for it) or do it yourself. From my hard earned experience, I decided to do it myself. It puts the control firmly in my hands and is a lot less expensive in many ways, but this is a choice on your part.

During the last few years, tools like blogs and other simple ways to launch a web presence have been developed. It's easier than ever now for an individual to launch quality work online.

Determine Your Topic

No one can be all things to all people. Some authors launch a hodgepodge of material which is a mixture of things only their immediate family would care about. They write for the broader public and maybe include a hobby or two thrown into the mix. Because that material is not targeted to a specific audience, it hits that target—no one. It's important when you launch your web presence that you determine your topic and stick with that topic.

Select a topic that is broad enough and something you have plenty of passion and things to say about—or at least find other quotes relating to that topic. If you stick to your topic and consistently build good content into your Web site, and promote it to everyone who crosses your path (using simple tools like a link in your email signature line), your audience will find you and come back to read what you have to say.

If you notice, each of the over 1,200 entries in my blog called The Writing Life are focused on writing and publishing. I've had other writers comment that they are amazed I don't veer from the topic but each one ties back into something about writing. That focus is intentional on my part and the consistency builds the audience. Readers know what they will find when they read my articles and content. It's important to select a theme and stay with that theme— no matter what other things you think you want to include on the site.

Four Places to Begin

It may seem daunting to launch a Web site. Here are some suggestions. I've used each of these tools and know they are effective to build a presence online.

Sitebuildit (www.buildit.sitesell.com/write2sell.html) is one of the best values online. You can build unlimited pages and use a huge user guide. This system does much more than build pages; it automatically gives you the ability to build your audience through the creation of a newsletter. Everything you need is in one economical price. I've built thousands of pages online with this system and it does not require that you know anything about the technical side of producing a Web site. It's where I built all of the pages in www.Right-Writing. com. Periodically I can change the design of the entire Web site with one command. It's remarkable, and I recommend you give serious consideration to this system.

Homestead (www.homestead.com) is another inexpensive system to consider for your building needs. It has simple template tools which are all point and click. You don't have to be a technical wizard or know much about computers to use these tools. In a short amount of time, you can create a professional site.

XsitePro (www.tinyurl.com/xsitepro2) is an inexpensive yet powerful Web site design program. Once again you don't have to have any technical computer know-how to design a well-crafted and professional Web site. With XsitePro, you need a hosting location such as Hostgator (www.tinyurl.com/hostgatr), which gives you a place on the Internet to put these professionally designed pages.

BlinkWeb (www.tinyurl.com/blnkweb) is a free and simple system for building a Web site with videos and click and use tutorials throughout.

These tools are just a few of the easy-to-use systems I recommend for building a web presence. It is important for you to begin some place and these will give you a starting point.

If you have not determined the topic for your web presence, then launch your own name as a Web site. Focus just on having some web pages that tell about you and your passion for writing and what you are doing. You never know when your name will pop into an editor's head and they will go to Google. What will they find? Give them something to discover about you. If you take control of the information and create it, it will be there. Every writer needs to jumpstart their presence on the Internet and build some pages.

Dig Deeper

1. Explore the four Web site resources mentioned in this chapter and see if any are right for your needs to build a web presence. Each of them is different.

2. Get a copy of *Web Marketing for Small Businesses, 7 Steps to Explosive Growth* by Stephanie Diamond (Sourcebooks, 2008) which contains excellent and current advice in this area of building a web presence.

3. Download and read this free 150-page Ebook about launching your own newsletter: www.terrylinks.com/E101

4. Go to www.terrylinks.com/rwnews and subscribe to *Right-Writing News*. As a part of your subscription, you will receive the free Ebook, *Emarketing Magic, How to Start Your Own Successful Newsletter or Ezine*. Read and study this valuable resource.

Awaken Your Dreams

1. Take time and create a plan to launch your own presence online. It will take time, thought, and energy but it will help you instantly gain credibility.

2. Launch a newsletter online and begin building your list of subscribers. You want to build the largest list you can build so regularly send information to the list with great content and people will be eager to receive your publication.

CHAPTER 14

Write Your Own Books

Every two years, the sports news is dominated by the Olympics. I have a slim writing connection to the Olympics because I wrote *Running On Ice* for Vonetta Flowers, the first African-American to win a gold medal in the 2002 Winter Olympics in Salt Lake City. Vonetta was a much decorated collegiate track and field athlete.

Several years ago, my phone rang and I met a two-time Olympian in track and field who had read *Running On Ice*. She loved Vonetta's book and wanted me to write her book. I often explore these writing opportunities with people. From hard-earned experience with folks who know almost nothing about publishing, I've learned to share a certain amount of education about the dynamics and competition in book publishing. After I give this information, they will decide if they want to work together or not.

In this case, I explained to this track and field star that I write some books but that 80 to 90 percent of nonfiction books are contracted on the basis of a nonfiction book proposal and a sample chapter or two. Publishers read book proposals and not book manuscripts.

This athlete explained because of her age and the point in her career, the 2008 games in China would be her last Olympics. Thus, we were discussing this possibility in a time frame in which the book proposal and sample chapter would have to be created in a short time period, then sent to various publishers so the book could be printed and released before the Summer Games. It's hard for inexperienced people to understand the short window of sales opportunity to market this specific type of book.

I write the book proposal and sample chapter for a negotiated fee. Then I write or ghostwrite the book upon a publisher's contract. Despite my experience and explanations about book publishing, this athlete balked at my fees for the project.

At that point in the process, I could have caved in and lowered my fees and probably received the work. Whenever I have taken a lower fee, I usually regret the results. My hard-earned experience told me to set the financial arrangements and if they worked, they worked. If not, then I wouldn't be the writer for this particular project.

Ultimately with this athlete, I wished her well with her book project and ended my back and forth communication. Several months ago, I received an email from her which announced her new book. I had no idea if she wrote it herself or found another writer. Ironically the book was self-published with a company which has one of the worst reputations for how they treat authors.

When the 2008 Summer Games in China began, I wondered if this athlete made the Olympic team as I wanted to cheer for her when the track and field events began. From my search, I learned she did not make it.

With various writing opportunities, you make the best possible decision at the time with the information you have, and then move ahead. I have been operating this way for years. The book publishing world is complex and there are many ways a simple decision can lead you down the wrong path. The challenge for each writer is to look at the options, get experienced wisdom, and then make the best possible decision. It is not easy.

The Problematic Incomplete Package

As I read the queries and pitches that come to me as an acquisitions editor, I'm continually amazed at the incomplete submissions—whether a one-page query letter or a book proposal and sample chapters or a fiction submission.

These writers want to get their book idea published, yet because they don't present a thorough, professional, and complete submission (query or proposal), then it's like they stand there and beg for rejection. Due to the volume of these submissions, I can almost guarantee they will receive a form rejection letter and nothing that explains that their idea was never fully considered because they were missing a piece of the puzzle.

For example, let's think about a recent query I received from a writer. After I read the pitch, I could not tell if it was fiction or nonfiction. So I asked—effort on my part to send a message. When I learned it was fiction, I asked an additional question: what type of fiction, young adult or adult? Also I asked about the length of the manuscript, specifically the word count. Otherwise, they will respond with the number of pages and cause more correspondence. Through a series of emails (which almost no acquisitions editor or literary agent will do), I learned this writer was pitching a 31,000 word novel.

Do you see the problem? It's not a full-length novel. This writer needs to return to her manuscript and add at least 20,000 additional words. Ironically, before she even approached me, she pitched a bunch of publishers who told her that they only took work from literary agents. Now she's pitching a bunch of literary agents and, in reality, she actually doesn't have anything to pitch because it is too short.

You may be one of those writers who has sent a submission to an editor or agent and haven't received an answer. You wonder why it takes so long to receive a response.

Here's one of the keys: Are you pitching a nonfiction book or fiction? If nonfiction, then you need a book proposal and several sample chapters before anyone will seriously consider your pitch. If you are pitching a novel, you need to have written the complete novel before you approach anyone about it. And you need to be enough of a student of the craft to understand the typical word count for your type of novel.

If you don't have any idea of the typical word count, then here are some general rules related to fiction word counts from best-selling novelist Lori Copeland:

Novella

20-25,000 words

80-100 pages

10-12 pages per chapter

Short Contemporary

50,000-60,000 words

200-240 pages

18-20 pages per chapter

Long Contemporary

70,000-80,000 words

280-320 pages

18-20 pages per chapter

Short Historical /Mainstream

90-100,000 words

360-400 pages

18-20 pages per chapter

Long Historical/ Mainstream

108,000-120,000

432-480 pages

18-20 pages per chapter

I encourage you to keep these word counts front and center because ignoring them is one of the easiest way to get a three-second rejection. You want to rejection-proof your submissions.

For your fiction to stand out from the other submissions, you will need to send a page-turning story (always key), a well-crafted synopsis, a short bio and, if you really want to show you understand the business of publishing, I recommend you also include a realistic plan which shows how you plan to help market your books. To sell books will involve conducting interviews with newspapers, magazines, and other media such as radio interviews. You also need to understand that journalists will need a nonfiction angle from your novel to talk with you. Otherwise they won't know what to ask you about your story. You want to show you understand their dilemma and are prepared for it.

I've rejected a great deal of fiction in recent months which was poorly crafted and poorly pitched. Also, in reality, there are fewer places to sell a fiction book than a nonfiction book. While we're talking about sales, the Authors Guild says a typical nonfiction book will sell 5,000 copies in the first year and a fiction book will sell 7,500 copies. These modest numbers may surprise you, especially when you realize you can write a 1500-word magazine article and easily reach 150,000 readers with many different print magazines.

Now let's turn to a nonfiction package. The key element with nonfiction is the visibility of the author to sell books, which is also called "the author's platform." Do you have this visibility, and is this visibility in the area you are pitching with this new project? For example, I recently read a women's leadership book. As I looked at the proposal and sample, I realized that the author had almost no visibility in the marketplace. She was trying to use her husband's platform as *her* platform, yet her husband was not a co-author in the book and his voice didn't appear in any of the chapters. In other words, it was a stretch and took seconds for me to spot. Any other agent or editor would also take only seconds to spot this flaw. This person needs to build her own platform before pitching the book idea. As I said earlier, publishers use authors' platforms; they do not build platforms for authors.

What is in a nonfiction book proposal? Most book proposals range from 15 to 30 pages, 100 percent typo-free, double-spaced with generous margins. The proposal takes many forms and the writer inevitably dictates its shape. The common elements include:

Overview. This area could be the most important part of your proposal and should be one to three pages long. In a succinct style it covers: What is the book about? Why is it necessary? Who is the audience? Who will buy this book? What makes the book different or better than any other book on this subject? What is the book's marketing handle? This is a 20-word-or-less description.

About the Author. Don't be shy. Why should the editor give you this project? Of everyone in the world why you? Show specifically why you are the most qualified individual for this project.

The Competition. Everyone believes their book is unique. It's not, so detail what other titles would be in direct competition. If you say there is no competition, you are practically begging for instant rejection.

Manuscript Delivery and Length. In the majority of cases, nonfiction books are not completed, so when can you deliver your manuscript and what will be the word count?

Promotion/ Special Markets/ Volume Buy Backs (anything over 5,000 copies). This portion of the proposal may be one of the most important because you will emphasize your ability to sell books. What can you do to help the book in terms of promotion?

Chapter Summaries. These summaries are an outline of the book. They can be as long as you desire but no less than 150 words for each chapter. Select the format that works best for you such as outline, narrative, or a bulleted list of key points.

Sample Chapters. You will need at least one sample chapter and probably two or three, if a chapter is less than ten pages. These chapters should give the editor a strong sense of the book's tone and style so make sure you show your best work.

I've gone into much greater detail about these elements in my how-to book called *Book Proposals That Sell, 21 Secrets to Speed Your Success*.

Make sure you have thought through the various key elements in your query and your longer submission—whether fiction or nonfiction. If you submit a complete package, your project will receive the consideration it deserves rather than instant rejection. It is only through the consideration process that you have any possibility of receiving the joyous email or phone call with a book offer from a publisher.

Like a Half-Marathon

I've never run a full marathon but I've thought about it several times during my life. At one point, I even purchased a marathon guidebook for a training schedule. For a multitude of excuses, I never managed to complete the marathon distance. At one point, I built my distance to where I ran a half-marathon distance—not in a race but on my own out on the road.

In many ways, writing full-length books is like running a half-marathon. You have to work at it consistently to finish. Through writing a bit each day, eventually you manage to complete the project. You can't push too hard or you will get exhausted and not finish. Also, if you think about the entire project from beginning to end, it becomes overwhelming at times and you will feel like quitting. Instead, you focus on the task for that particular day such as completing a chapter or part of a chapter, and then on another day you complete the next chapter. It's not a sprint or short race but a lengthy effort.

Recently I felt exhilaration when I finished another book-length manuscript. I had written part of this manuscript last year. Over the last few weeks, I've been working hard to expand it, rework the sentences, and add new stories along with current how-to information and statistics. My overall goal was to expand the content about 30 percent from its former size. When I completed my planned additions, I counted my words and was pleased to discover that unconsciously I had written to my overall goal.

I printed the entire manuscript and gave it one last read before I sent it off. What a relief to have this project in the hands of a capable editor. I'll have to go through another round of revision (or two or three). It's the editorial process—even for much published writers and editors like me. I want to always continue to grow in my craft and be open to revision and changes. It's one of the pure signs of a professional from my view. While I'm aware there will be more work ahead for this particular project, I'm relieved to have completed this part of the process.

I'm unsure where you are in the writing journey. Maybe you are wondering if you can even write. Or maybe you write magazine articles and are wondering if you can complete a book. You never know if you don't try.

Have you fallen for the big lie that writers are born? Or maybe you believe you either have it or you don't have it and it can't be taught? It will encourage you to begin that half-marathon book project you have been thinking about and chip away at it until you complete it.

In the opening for this chapter, I mentioned writing *Running On Ice* by Vonetta Flowers, the first African-American to win a gold medal in the Winter Olympics. While admittedly, I'm not the most athletic person you will ever meet, as I wrote this book, I learned quite a bit about the process. In fact, I wrote this book in six weeks and had a crash course in bobsledding. Vonetta was a much decorated collegiate track and field star who believed her quest for Olympic gold was over with the Sacramento trials for the 2000 Sydney Games. Then her husband, Johnny, spotted a flyer encouraging the athletes to try out for the bobsled. Living in Birmingham, Alabama, the Flowers' only connection to bobsledding was the Disney movie *Cool Runnings* about the Jamaican bobsled team. With little faith that anything would happen, Vonetta tried out and discovered that her years in track and field paid off. She had the perfect set of skills for bobsledding and has become a top brakeman and won a gold medal. From writing Vonetta's story, I had the opportunity to hold her gold medal. It was an unforgettable experience.

I've learned the search for gold isn't only in an Olympic setting. It is actively happening in editorial offices. Editors are looking for the next bestseller or at least a book that will find its audience. Some books are slow at first, and then gradually increase in sales. These books may or may not appear on a "best-seller list" but their consistent sales are a key part of the publisher's goals. If you haven't read it, I highly recommend Michael Korda's *Making the List: A Cultural History of a Bestseller*. The former editor-in-chief at Simon and Schuster examines the best-seller lists from the last century with surprising results. Publishers use their experience with past books to create marketing plans and publicity campaigns. Their sales reps travel around the country to sell them to bookstores. The search for gold, or best-selling books, is long and hard.

I am constantly sorting through nonfiction and fiction proposals, rejecting most of them. I dislike sending back these proposals but it's part of the business—and always remember that it is business and not personal. I know that's hard to understand because you get so much of yourself wrapped into your project.

As an editor, I'm always gathering information about publishing, books, and authors, and that information comes into play as I sort through these proposals. When I was a fiction acquisitions editor, I read an excellent proposal from an author who had sold over 500,000 novels. This type of sales history catches an editor's attention when combined with an interesting plot premise. One of the hardest things to see in these proposals is something that isn't there. It's the same with proofreading and other parts of this business. Missing elements are glossed over and often ignored. For this fiction author, I recalled her extensive personal marketing efforts for her last novel. She had organized her own author tour with book signings and media events in numerous cities, yet she had included none of this information in her proposal. I picked up the telephone and called her agent who confirmed my memory of this effort. The agent was going to have this author prepare some details about her personal marketing efforts which I could use to supplement her proposal. This supplemental material would be important when I pitched the project to the publication board. Then I dug out some additional information which wasn't in her proposal.

In general, a literary agent simultaneously submits proposals to different publishers. If as an editor, I was able to add something to a presentation or a proposal, it would present the project in a completely different light to my publishing colleagues. It's one of the ways as an acquisitions editor and a former literary agent that I'm looking for gold.

Always make sure your proposals and pitches to editors and literary agents are complete. To the best of your ability, make each line sizzle and snap with an irresistible siren that says, "Publish me." It's not easy. It involves a lot of work and effort, but it *is* possible.

Dig Deeper

1. I've written an Ebook with more insight about how to catch an editor's attention called *Straight Talk from the Editor, 18 Keys to a Rejection-Proof Submission.* You can get this book free at: www.straighttalkeditor.com.

2. Also for in-depth insight about the book world, I recommend you take my Write A Book Proposal online course (www.WriteABookProposal.com) Through 12-lessons, I guide you step-by-step how to write a complete book proposal. Also I have a free teleseminar about proposal creation at: www.AskAboutProposals.com.

3. In addition, I recommend you study *Book Proposals That Sell, 21 Secrets to Speed Your Success*—available from Amazon (with over 100 Five Star reviews) or the Ebook version at: www.bookproposals.ws.

4. Finally, I've collected even more information about book proposal creation into another free Ebook, *Book Proposals That Sell, Extra Special Report* which you can get at: www.bookproposalcoach.com.

Awaken Your Dreams

1. What plans do you have to write books? Have you written a proposal? Take a moment to write down your specific goals in this area.

2. Periodically look at your goals and see how they have changed or need to change. Our dreams change as we accomplish one part of them or enter a different phase in our writing life.

CHAPTER 15

Capture the Stories of Others

The blonde-haired writer sat across from me during a writer's conference, leaned into the table, and poured out her frustration. She had a journalism degree, spent her season working for newspapers, and now had published a series of magazine articles. At first the publications had modest pay but now this writer was beginning to write for higher paying and more well-known publications.

Yet she revealed her book ideas were rejected and she understood the reasons. In the nonfiction areas, she had no "platform" or market visibility. While her standing was rising among magazine editors, she recognized that few readers knew her and her work.

This writer had dreams of writing a novel but had realistically looked at the market and understood the huge hurdles she faced to get a novel published. While she could spin an excellent tale, she wondered how she could devote the time and energy to writing an 80,000 to 100,000 word novel with the speculation that some publisher "might" bring it into print. She had no interest in self-publishing and producing a garage filled with books that never reached readers.

Now during our brief session, this writer was searching for answers about how to break into book publishing. She wanted to write longer works than magazine articles, but was unsure where to turn.

If the story sounds familiar to you, then keep reading because I'm going to show you a forgotten path for book publishing. This path has endless possibilities and can provide financial security and a lifetime of publishing.

If you don't have a platform, one of the quickest ways to gain one is to use the platform of someone else. This is called co-authoring or ghostwriting. If you don't personally lead a large organization, can you write for someone who does? I call it the forgotten path as many of these busy people have aspirations of writing a book but will never get it done because of their own schedule. Yet they could make time to meet with a writer on a regular basis, tell you the stories, and allow you to write the book for them. The writer doesn't have to have the platform but instead brings the skill of crafting words and storytelling to the project.

Many years ago I discovered that I have a finite number of books that I want to write during my lifetime, yet there are also an infinite number of books I can co-author or ghostwrite for someone else.

If you have never tried co-authoring or ghostwriting, I suggest you try a magazine article for your first experience. It is better to experiment with a shorter assignment than a longer book project. Can you capture another person's stories and voice? Are you willing to be a co-author or a ghostwriter as long as you are fairly compensated for your work?

You can often find these longer book projects by writing a shorter magazine article. I started my relationship with someone through a magazine article, and now it has developed into a book project. I've seen many other writers have this same experience in which they get with a high-profile person to write a magazine article. This starts their relationship, then that relationship takes a leap to a new level and they become co-authors for a longer book project.

From my experience, it is rare for an agent or an editor to put a high profile person with an inexperienced co-author or ghostwriter. You can gain the necessary experience collaborating on shorter magazine articles, and then in the future you might become their writer for a book.

Through my collaboration and co-author experiences, I've been able to write about some remarkable people who are now my friends. It has enriched my life and provided work. I hope you will consider this forgotten path.

For Your Personal Growth

I've taught on this topic of ghostwriting or co-authoring at various writers' conferences. At one large conference, I had less than half a dozen people at my workshop. Many people want to write books but they want to write their own books and not books for someone else.

I've also met many authors who co-authored one book and vowed never to do it again. Co-authoring is a relational challenge for the writer because you are not operating in isolation. Instead you have to serve the other person and be intent on getting their story and their words into print. I've ghostwritten or co-authored more than a dozen books. There are several reasons to do it.

There was something in her writing for just about anyone.

The first reason is the big need in the market for people who can write the stories of others. As a co-author, I've visited the floor of the Chicago Mercantile Exchange and stood right there with the traders, and I've put on a helmet and ridden a bobsled down a mountain. Each of these experiences contributed to being able to write material for my co-author and complete a book project. You can write an endless number of books through the eyes of someone else. These people may not have your writing skills or they may be simply too busy to produce a manuscript.

Second, as a writer you can make a good living writing the stories of others. My first collaboration book project was with Chris Woehr called *One Bright Shining Path, Faith in the Midst of Terrorism* (Crossway Books). In the early '90s, the Shining Path brutally killed a national translator in Peru, South America. At the time, I was the manager of the editorial department at Wycliffe Bible Translators and in charge of their books, magazine, and printed materials. I felt this dynamic story had to appear in a book format and I was looking to find the best writer for the project.

I called best-selling author Philip Yancey and asked him to write this book for Wycliffe. He knew about the story and was interested but had a busy writing schedule. The year before he had interrupted his work to write a book about the Russian church, and he was determined not to interrupt his writing schedule again. He was polite but said no. I continued to rack my brain to determine who could write this book.

At that time, the company headquarters was located a mile and a half from the beach in Southern California. I went out for my lunchtime run, and during that time I reflected on my own experiences in Peru and that part of the world. I had never written a full-length adult book, yet I had been to this part of the world, and I could taste the dust on those roads so I could describe it to the reader. I felt like I could be the writer for this book. Chris Woehr and I combined our talents for this project. Because she was bi-lingual in Spanish, she traveled to Peru and did the interviews, gathering the stories and the content. Then she translated and transcribed the interviews and sent the material to me. I wrote the book from her information and for many years, Crossway Books kept the story in print. At times during the writing process, this book looked impossible to create. The work was hard—in fact, none of my books have been easy—even though going into them I'm optimistically thinking they will be easy. Each one takes a lot of energy and hard work.

The Unexpected Mentor

I loved to come into my California office on a Sunday afternoon. At the time, I had small children at home and I found it hard to write and meet some of my freelance deadlines. So I would often slip off to the office for a few afternoon hours. To give you the right time frame, it was in the mid-'80s and I rode a Honda Scooter back and forth from home to the office.

On one of these Sunday afternoons, when I came into the building, I noticed the lights on in the director's office, and because everything else was still, I walked past to see what was happening. Jamie Buckingham, a friend of the director, was sitting at the keyboard. He looked up and greeted me and said, "I'm a jungle pilot today flying planes in the Amazon." The writer of such bestsellers as *Run Baby Run* by Nicky Cruz, Jamie was a prolific writer and yet a couple of times a year, he wrote some material that never carried his byline and didn't pay a dime. As a pure ghostwriting ministry, Jamie wrote all of the public material from our director.

When readers would rave to me about the director's engaging storytelling, I would always smile and say, "Yes, the writing is terrific." I knew the director didn't write any of it; the words came from Jamie's pen.

Many readers might not remember Jamie Buckingham but millions of people are still reading his writing and his ghostwriting. He was a favorite columnist for *Charisma* magazine and died of liver cancer in 1992. I learned a great deal from his life and his teaching about writing—through his words and through his actions.

Here's a story that few people remember about Jamie but I write it to encourage you about second chances. Dean Merrill wrote this story in a little book from Zondervan published in 1981 called *Another Chance, How God Overrides Our Big Mistakes* (long out of print but you can get as an inexpensive used book). On page 59, Merrill includes an excerpt from Buckingham's *Where Eagles Soar*, "Well-known author and speaker Jamie Buckingham describes how God painfully confronted him with a sin—not once but twice. He was a successful pastor in his mid-thirties at the time, but only after this canyon of embarrassment did his wider ministry as a writer emerge."

In October 1965, a group of 20 deacons in a large Baptist church in South Carolina confronted Buckingham with stern faces. They forced his resignation, and he writes about calling his wife and asking her to come get him at the church.

> She found me, the shepherd of the flock, crouched in a fetal position in a basement hallway, huddled against the landing of the stairs. "It would be better for you, for this church if I were dead," I sobbed. She comforted. She smoothed. She never asked for details. There was no need....There was a desperate reaching out for friends, only to find they had all deserted. I was like a leper. Unclean. I wrote letters—more than 90 of them—to pastoral and denominational friends. Only one man dared respond and that was with a curt, "I received your letter and shall be praying for you."

The Buckinghams returned to his home state of Florida and led a small but growing church. "But as Vance Havner once remarked, It doesn't do any good to change labels on an empty bottle. Nothing inside me had changed. I was still the magnificent manipulator, the master of control, the defender of my position. I was still pushing people around. I was far more politician than a man of God....Soon echoes from the past began drifting down to Florida...I continued to fight, to brave the growing onslaught of fact that kept building against me. It took 15 months of a stormy relationship before the Florida church cast me into the waves to calm the sea—just like Jonah....I had no choice but once again to slink home and huddle with my wife and children while the fire of God continued its purging work. Often, I have discovered, we cannot hear God when we are busy. Hearing comes only when we have taken—or are forced to take— times of quietness.

In his idleness, Jamie picked up a copy of *Guideposts* and learned about their first contest for writers. He submitted a first-person 1,500 word story about a young man who prepared to go to South America as a missionary pilot. "Since I had nothing else to do, I wrote the story and sent it in. On October 1, 1967, I was stretched out on the bed in the back room of our little rented house when the phone rang. It was the Western Union telegraph office. Jackie took the call and copied the message on a scrap of paper. It was from Leonard LeSourd, editor of *Guideposts*, stating I was one of the 20 winners—out of more than 2,000 submissions."

At that workshop, Jamie learned more about how to write the stories of others, and here he also met the publisher who was looking for someone to write *Run Baby Run* for Nicky Cruz. His career as a ghostwriter and co-author was born.

It was my privilege for those few years to see Jamie on a regular basis and watch him work. He even taught a several day writer's workshop for our staff during the early days of my own writing life. It was long before I co-authored any books with anyone. Looking back, I see that in many ways Jamie served as the unexpected role model for this part of my writing life.

That experience launched my writing books for other people. Since that first book, I've had many different experiences with co-authoring. I wrote *Lessons From the Pit* (B & H Publishing Group) by Joe Leininger who traded for ten years in the Eurodollar Pit of the Chicago Mercantile. I wrote a diet book called *First Place* (Regal

Books) which has over 100,000 copies in print by Carole Lewis. And I even rode a bobsled down the mountain in the Olympic Park in Utah to gain experience for writing Vonetta Flowers' *Running On Ice*.

Sometimes these books are written for a straight fee. Other times I split the money with the author. This division of funds can vary widely in percentages depending on what is negotiated. The most typical split is a 50/50 split between the writer and the personality. I would encourage you to negotiate details such as division of labor, financial arrangements, and the way your name appears on the book, at the beginning stages of your relationship with your co-author. This is the absolute best time for this give-and-take negotiation. Once the two of you agree on these arrangements, then you should formalize this agreement with a simple letter, dated and in duplicate—one for each party. You can use a literary attorney to formalize this agreement or simply create the letter between yourself and your co-author. This agreement should also clarify how you dissolve your relationship and what type of notification is necessary (typically at least 30 days for either party). In these early stages of working together it's always difficult to know how the relationship will go and you want to have a way of handling any difficulties. I've learned the hard way that not everything ends up as rosy as projected in the early days.

Dig Deeper

1. *Ghostwriters from the Inside Out* is a free Ebook you can receive instantly if you go to this site: www.terrylinks.com/jump and register. Also you receive *eBook Marketing Revealed.* These two free Ebooks are valued at $84.

2. Another excellent resource I recommend on this topic is *Ghost-Writing For Fun & Profit* by Eva Shaw, Ph.D. (Writeriffic Publishing Group, 2003). Dr. Shaw has ghostwritten books for over thirty years and readers of this comprehensive title gain the benefit of her experience, teaching, and insight. This book gives you step-by-step insight from a seasoned professional. It's one of the rarely discussed aspects of book publishing—yet potentially one of the easiest ways for a writer to make a solid living. You don't need a "platform" or a huge audience to be the writer for someone else—or their ghost. Whether you get your name on the cover of the book or not, ghostwriters fill a huge need in the publishing industry and practice their craft as servants of the story.

3. *Write a Book Without Lifting a Finger, How to Hire a Ghostwriter Even if You're on a Shoestring Budget* by Mahesh Grossman (10 Finger Press, 2004) Even if you never plan on hiring a ghostwriter but would like to get a book published, get this title. It includes information, stories, quotations, and detail that I've never seen in a printed form. Grossman knows what it takes to get a book deal and how to create a focused book proposal which will stand out from everything else and land the attention of a major publisher.

4. *How to Write with a Collaborator* by Hal Zina Bennett with Michael Larsen (Writer's Digest Books, 1988)—part of the Writer's Basic Bookshelf series and one of the only books available on this topic. Contains sample collaboration agreements, ghostwriter agreement, agent agreement, publishing contracts, and other helpful stories and advice. This book is excellent, but out of print so track it down through your local library or a used bookstore.

5. *Business & Legal Forms for Authors & Self-Publishers* by Tad Crawford (Allworth Press, 2005). While this particular book is broader than the topic of co-authoring, it includes collaboration agreements and checklists of points to consider and is an overall excellent resource. It is still in print and available. The third edition of this book includes a CD with all of the forms on it.

Awaken Your Dreams

1. What types of stories would you like to write for someone else? Plan to query several publications and get an assignment to write these articles. The assignment will allow you to reach experts or celebrities. Each time, make a point to mention to the expert your availability to co-author with them on a longer project. Just opening the door of conversation may lead to additional opportunities. Follow the old saying, "It won't fly if you don't try."

CHAPTER 16

Advance Your Career with a Literary Agent

"They are doing what?" I took a deep breath and then asked my agent for some additional information. A major publisher was cancelling a six-figure book deal I was writing. Over the previous months, I had spent hours writing my manuscript, along with spending two weeks of my life in a small city in Oklahoma working with my co-author. Now in one sweeping motion, the legal team of this publisher had notified my literary agent that the book was cancelled and demanded the return of the advance which was long spent.

I was thankful that I did not have to face this situation alone. Instead my New York literary agent was able to handle the situation. We didn't have to return the advance; however, my book project disappeared and has never appeared in print.

During over 20 years in publishing, I've seen many things go wrong as a book manuscript winds its way toward publication. Your editor leaves the publishing house and your book has no internal champion. You can't connect with anyone about your manuscript—by phone or email. Or you have a difference of opinion between yourself and the editor about the shape of the manuscript, cover, or any number of other factors.

Let your imagination run wild in this area of potential problems on the path to publishing a book. The majority of the time, books wind their way toward publication without any challenges but if there is a bump, do you stand alone or do you have a skilled literary agent in your corner?

I wrote over 40 books with traditional publishers before obtaining a literary agent. Not every writer needs an agent and, in practice, it is often more difficult to find a good agent than to get published in the first place. In fact, I recommend most writers write several books before they sign with an agent; however, in today's publishing world that is not always possible.

As I've mentioned in other parts of this book, there is a high volume of material in circulation at publishing houses. *Dan Poynter's Self-publishing Manual* says,

It has been estimated that more than 2 million book-length manuscripts are circulated to publishers each year and many of the large publishers receive 3,000 to 5,000 unsolicited manuscripts each week. Reading all these manuscripts would take an enormous amount of time, and a high percentage of the submissions do not even fit the publisher's line. They are a waste of editorial time. Consequently, many of the publishers refuse delivery of unsolicited manuscripts by rubber-stamping the packages "Return to Sender"; writers are being rejected without being read![19]

Many publishers have closed their doors to unsolicited or "over the transom" submissions. In the publishing world, this stack of submissions is known as a slush pile. It is well-named from my view because to find something good in that stack is like panning for gold in a stream that rarely has anything golden. Editors and agents go through stacks of material before they find anything of value.

One well-known publisher told me about receiving over 6,000 of these unsolicited submissions during a 12-month period which the staff devoted considerable time and effort to read and process. The editorial director called for an accounting from this work and asked, "Did they issue any book contracts from these 6,000 submissions?"

The answer: no. Not a single book was contracted from this volume of submissions. This makes it clear that publishers have many other ways of finding new authors rather than reading through unsolicited material. Acquisitions editors are actively courting authors who are published with other companies. These editors also read magazines and newspapers, track culture trends, and listen to speakers at conferences, then approach the speakers for books. It's a good reality check for writers to realize that no one is "waiting" for your book idea to come to the publishing house. It's why you have to "prove" the value of your idea through a book proposal.

These policies from the publishers mean you can no longer write to the editor directly and send in your proposal or manuscript. If the publisher has this policy of not reading unsolicited manuscripts, your submission will be returned unopened and unread. You may get around it, however, by attending a conference and meeting an editor face-to-face, and then follow up by mail.

As recently as ten years ago, many of the major authors did not have a literary agent to represent them. Today most of the best-selling authors have someone to represent their business efforts. While there are some unscrupulous agents, in general agents work on a percentage basis or a commission. If they don't sell your work, they are not paid for their efforts. The typical agent receives 15 percent to 20 percent on domestic book contracts and 20 percent on foreign rights sales. (In general foreign rights sales are not large dollar amounts.) Under this publishing system, the typical literary agent has to be cautious about first-time or relatively new book authors who don't have a large sales track record. Until an author has built a large following or platform, the typical hard-working agent is going to be reluctant to take a risk on them as a client. It's a risk because they may work back and forth on a concept, send it out to many publishers, track the rejections, and not earn anything for their efforts. Literary agents (and editors) are actively looking for projects with a built-in audience and which are well-written for an almost "guaranteed" sale. While authors with a sales track record can get a literary agent, it's hard for the beginning book author. Don't be frustrated if you don't immediately find one.

If you have a literary agent, then you have someone else who negotiates the financial terms of your book contract. Using an agent makes the process less confrontational than doing it face-to-face. An agent can ask for certain terms in your contract that you, as the writer, are reluctant to request. An agent also gives career advice and helps guide you through any difficulties in the process of working with your publisher. Plus, they also review your book royalty statement and contact the publisher in the rare instance any matters require resolution.

One major caution in this area: Anyone can hang out a shingle and become an agent. It's the author's responsibility to ask questions and see if this person is a good match for *his* goals as a writer. Writers are often over-eager to find a literary agent and I would advise that while you can often learn a great deal from an agent, never forget that the agent works for you. Sometimes I've seen writers reverse the roles and wrongly believe they are working for the agent. Instead, remember you are paying the agent from the commissions as your work sells to a publisher.

Some literary agents who advertise in writing magazines charge reading fees. To learn how literary agents can prey on unpublished authors, read Jim Fisher's book, *Ten Percent of Nothing, The Case of the Literary Agent from Hell* (www.snipurl.com/tenper) (Southern Illinois University Press, 2004). Fisher is a former FBI agent and this book reads like a fascinating novel. You will learn about a frustrated science fiction novelist, Dorothy Deering, who was burned by two fee-charging literary agents who did nothing to locate a publisher for her work. As an ex-con, Dorothy saw the money-making potential in starting her own fee-based agency. She believed there were thousands of writers who had dreams about book publishing yet couldn't get the attention of traditional publishers. These writers would be willing to pay money to have their work marketed to publishers. This simple concept of fee-based reading and marketing of manuscripts began one of the biggest scams in American publishing history.

Thousands of would-be writers paid millions of dollars to Deering, a former bookkeeper who had no professional experience as a writer, editor, agent, or publisher. Fisher, who worked for the FBI for over 20 years, was drawn to this story after learning of a friend who lost money in this scam. The author exposes an ugly side of American publishing and the book emphasizes the warning signs to any would-be writer so they will not be drawn into such practices.

Dorothy Deering never sold a single manuscript to a major publisher, and the money she bilked from her clients was spent on personal cruises and expensive cars and homes. In one of the few "agent like" activities in this book, Deering and her husband travel to New York City and bring a huge stack of their clients' manuscripts. The pair walked into the lobby of a mainstream publisher and called an editor downstairs to meet with them. After greeting the editor, Deering pointed to the large stack of paper and said, "Here you go." It was all the pitch the editor received about the paperwork as the couple walked out the front door. The editor boxed up the paperwork and mailed it to them with a note saying they should never send them anything again. This small action is the most proactive step the Dorothy Deering Literary Agency of Nicholasville, Kentucky, takes throughout this entire book. For her scam to writers, Dorothy Deering was sentenced to ten years in prison but others have taken up this confidence game in publishing and writers need to know about this little-talked-about aspect.

As an editor and a writer, I worked with a number of terrific agents. It's interesting to me the depth we go to when we check out a good car dealership, yet how we don't do our due diligence with an agent. I understand part of it. As writers, we'll select anyone who wants our work, but that might not be the wisest route. Anyone can become an agent and that agent might not be the right one for you.

The Association of Authors Representatives (www.aar-online.org) includes a detailed list of starter questions to ask your prospective agent:

- How long have you been in business as an agent?

- Do you have specialists at your agency who handle movie and television rights? Foreign rights?

- Who in your agency will actually be handling my work?

- Will the other staff members be familiar with the status of my business at your agency?

- Will you oversee or at least keep me apprised of the work that your agency is doing on my behalf?

- Do you issue an agent-author agreement?

- May I review the language of the agency clause that appears in contracts you negotiate for your clients?

- How do you keep your clients informed of your activities on their behalf?

- Do you consult with your clients on any and all offers?

- What are your commission rates?

- What are your procedures and time-frames for processing and disbursing client funds?

- Do you keep different bank accounts separating author funds from agency revenue?

- What are your policies about charging clients for expenses incurred by your agency?

These questions will give you some idea of the types of issues that you should consider before signing with any agent. And every agent should be willing to answer these questions if they want you to sign with their agency. Another excellent resource is an article from Victoria Strauss containing many links and solid information (www. terrylinks.com/safest).

Agents perform a variety of functions for their clients. Some just sell the proposal to a particular publisher. Good agents, however, often function as an editor for their clients, returning the proposal with suggestions about how to reshape it to increase the chance of a sale. Agents must understand contractual law and how to negotiate with publishers on behalf of their clients. They also negotiate other rights such as foreign rights, film, TV, and audio, and help their clients with their long-term strategy in the market.

Many agents are former book editors; thus, they understand the details of a profit and loss (P & L) statement, or the actual book financials that the author never sees. The specifics of these numbers are important for determining the author's advance. The higher the print run, the larger the advance for the book but publishers want to print the minimum amount of books which will sell during the first year of publication; otherwise, they have a warehouse problem. The P & L drives many of the internal decisions within the publishing house. These editors-turned-agents have sat inside the publishing houses. They've seen what it takes to produce a bestseller, and they understand the pressures and struggles that beset editors. When there is a problem with the manuscript or any number of other things in the process of working with an author, the editor often turns to the agent first.

I completely understand how writers land bad agents. You get a phone call or a letter from someone who wants to see your work. They have seen your Web site, read one of your magazine articles, or in some way have received your name and contact information. You leap with excitement at the thought of getting an agent, but I recommend you thoroughly check out each potential publishing partner. Each of us, as writers, is insecure about our writing and the merits of our idea or book proposal. Yes, our family loves it, but what about the publishing world? From my years in publishing I have learned that while no one enjoys getting rejected, it's a key part of this occupation. Some of our ideas find a home and others are repeatedly rejected. The journey to book publishing is different for each person. Cultivating and seeking relationships with literary agents and editors is a critical part of the publishing business. As

John Kremer, the author of *1001 Ways to Market Your Book,* has said, "Publishing is about relationships."

What characterizes a bad agent? According to Eckstut and Sterry,

> Bad agents won't return your phone calls and sometimes even steal your money. Like bad travel agents, they can send you on some really bad trips, or worse, not even get you off the ground. Naturally, there are many more bad agents than good agents. Sadly, when you meet them, it's often hard to tell the difference. But once you've experienced their incompetence, sloth and/or idiocy firsthand, the distinction becomes painfully obvious.[20]

If I have an agent, does that eliminate the need for an attorney with my book contract? Like most of these questions in publishing, the answer begins with "It depends…" Each situation is different so it's hard to make generalities but here are some basics to understand. An agent may know contract law and, in a few cases, is also an attorney, but not in the majority of cases.

While many agents are excellent in their negotiations, understand that in any publishing situation, the agent can only push the negotiations so far—then they back off or risk stretching their relationship with the publisher. Everyone—the publisher, the agent, and the author—is looking for a fair agreement. Each party's interest and perspective will be different for each contract.

Authors need to remember that the agent's name is not at the bottom of the book contract—it's the author's name. Having an agent involved doesn't necessarily exclude the involvement of an attorney. You may still want to get one to check your contract and give you some feedback about it. There are many specialties of lawyers but only a literary lawyer knows the details related to publishing contract law.

Where do you find a literary attorney? One of the best resources is the Authors Guild (www.authorsguild.org). They regularly review book contracts for their members and will help you understand the details. As an acquisitions editor for a publishing house, I explain the contract to authors and clarify its terms. Because I worked for the publisher, however, I do not give the author any advice about how to improve the terms of this contract. The contracts originate with the publisher and are always written in their best interest. As the author, you need to find someone to evaluate your contract with your concerns as their primary interest.

Whenever you get to this point in the publishing process, take the time to celebrate. As an editor, I know that I've gone through a lot of internal effort to get to the place where I can offer a writer a book contract. Book publishing is a consensus building process. A number of publishing executives have to be convinced about a project before a contract can be issued. The negotiations include some give and take. Sometimes they end up in a "deal breaker" in which the deal falls apart. But normally the author, the agent, and the publisher negotiate with the idea of coming to a fair compromise for everyone involved. It's an exciting part of the process to be offered a book contract—no matter how many books you have published.

Agents are definitely a part of the writing landscape and they are here to stay. Because the agent often increases the offer for the author, their addition has not always been well received and I've been in meetings where the publishers have complained about their presence. Yet overall, agents have helped the communication process between authors and publishers, and most provide a great service to the publishers with quality submissions.

My Warning Bells Sounded

The package looked innocent when it arrived—a USPS priority mail package addressed to me when I was a fiction acquisitions editor. I opened it and my internal warning bells sounded.

First, it was a bound manuscript. Again, this wasn't too unusual. Sometimes a fiction author will produce a Print On Demand version or self-publish their novel and be interested in a traditional publisher acquiring the book for a broader distribution.

Then I noticed the cover letter came from a literary agent—someone I didn't recognize. Again, that's not too unusual because anyone can hang out an agent shingle. Many people are getting into the agent business including former editors.

With this agent's cover letter, the warning bells sounded. I think it was the phrases about a "compilation of prayer and insightful prose" and "to guide readers along a path to spiritual enlightenment." Then the next sentence claimed the book "appeals to readers of any faith."

OK, I thought. *Let's check it out.*

Louder warning bells sounded. Large typeface (helps you produce a larger book than would normally happen). Every page was a one-page chapter of a thought or prayer and the bound book was published by an outfit that I've seen numerous complaints about on some online groups. I'd never seen an actual book from this outfit—until now.

Over the last few years, I've opened thousands of these submissions—but I'd never seen a package like this one. I looked a bit closer at the author information. Her first book and she's working on a second book (admirable).

Then I thought I'd check for some more information about the agent. (Writers should listen up here. I'm going to teach you how to fish—for information). First, I went to Everyone Who's Anyone In Trade Publishing (www.everyonewhosanyone.com). This page has a search engine and I entered the first and last name. Nothing. Then I entered only the last name and searched. Again nothing. I entered the first name and searched. Nothing.

Next I turned to the Association of Author's Representatives home page (www.aar-online.org) which has a search engine feature for their database. Again I looked for this agent's name. Nothing. The fact this agent was not listed was not too unusual because not every agent is a member of the AAR. Many of the Christian literary agents that I worked with on a regular basis are not members.

Finally I tried a Google search on the person's name. I found nothing; not everyone in publishing is on the Internet. I searched my own name "Terry Whalin" and in 0.25 seconds, Google found 3,700 results with the first few entries accurate and you could learn my background. It sounded more warning bells.

I sent this "literary agent" my standard form rejection letter, and then logged some details into my fiction manuscript log. The experience bothered me for the author who is obviously putting some effort and energy into getting her project into the marketplace.

Each of us as writers desires someone to want our material. It's admirable as we pursue our dreams of publication (and sales) that someone comes along who wants to be our literary agent. It's our responsibility as the author, however, to check out the agent and make wise decisions.

Great Agent, Good Agent, or Bad Agent

Literary agents are an ongoing discussion within the book publishing community. Various online groups will discuss it. When they get together on the phone or in person, editors will talk about agents. Recently, I was talking with one long-time literary agent who mentioned a common misconception. Agents do not work for a particular publishing house. They may only have a lot of dealings with a particular publishing house if the publisher acquires the books from the agent's clients.

The book *The Essential Guide to Getting Your Book Published,* by Arielle Eckstut and David Henry Sterry, includes a chapter called "Locating, Luring and Landing the Right Agent" which is filled with insight and wisdom. Arielle is a literary agent with the Levine Greenberg Literary Agency. From that vantage point, these authors describe the qualities of a good agent, qualities of a great agent, and also include some of the characteristics of a bad agent. They also discuss whether you need an agent in the first place and how to determine the answer to your situation.

The great agent is a true partner with the author and as Eckstut and Sterry write, "*Great* agents are part wizard, midwife and guide dog. They'll show you the tricks of the trade, manage your career, introduce you to all the right people, and guide you and your manuscript through the messy maze of the modern book world."[21] My experience matches these characteristics and I've worked with some great agents who know how to carefully guide me through the various land mines of publishing. It's the responsibility of the writer to follow a principle emphasized repeatedly in this book: research, research, research.

I've Fired a Couple of Agents

During my years as a writer, I've hired a number of different literary agents and worked with them. In a few cases, I've also terminated my relationship with some. We parted as friends, however, because it is important in the small world of publishing never to burn relationship bridges.

I included these details in this chapter about agents because I want you to see the importance of finding the right one for your writing. It may involve you signing with one agent and working with that individual for a while, then making a change to someone else. I often compare the agent relationship to dating and marriage. It's important for you to find the right fit. This will involve asking many questions and learning what you need from an agent, then finding that right individual. There are many possibilities in today's market and you will need to choose with care. I wish you well in the search.

Dig Deeper

1. There are many excellent literary agents. To give you a starting point, I'm offering this free list of over 400 agents with names, agency address, and contact information: www.terrylinks.com/agents

2. Michael Larsen is the cofounder of the Larsen/Pomeda Agency, one of California's oldest literary agencies. He has written *How to Get a Literary Agent* (Sourcebooks, 2006) www.snipurl.com/litagent which is packed with insight.

3. Rick Frishman and Robyn Freedman Spitzman have written *Author 101 Bestselling Secrets From Top Agents, The Insider's Guide to What Agents and Publishers Really Want* (Adams Media, 2006) and I recommend this resource as another way to learn more detailed information about this topic of agents.

4. A book which is almost a classic in this area is *How to Be Your Own Literary Agent* by Richard Curtis (Houghton Mifflin, 2003). This top literary agent writes this easy-to-read book with clarity and authority. It has been revised several times.

5. *The Essential Guide to Getting Your Book Published* by Arielle Eckstut and David Henry Sterry (Workman, 2010) w w w . amzn.to/Up9wvO is much more than about agents but includes a comprehensive chapter on this matter.

6. *Making the Perfect Pitch, How to Catch a Literary Agent's Eye* by Katharine Sands (Watson-Guptill, 2004) collects wisdom from a number of different agents into a single excellent volume.

7. *The Publishing Game: Find an Agent in 30 Days* by Fern Reiss (Peanut Butter and Jelly Press, 2003). www.snipurl.com/agentin30 Step-by-step advice and a 30 days plan on what it takes for any writer to land an agent. This book is excellent.

Awaken Your Dreams

1. Where are you with your dreams of getting a book published? Take a few moments to consider your present situation and set some goals for the future.

2. Take active steps to begin a relationship with several different agents. You might not have anything to present to them yet but begin building the relationship today. Then in the future when you are ready to make a pitch, you will be prepared with a plan.

CHAPTER 17

Remember the Children

When my sons were small, I made weekly treks to the local library. In the children's area, we checked out stacks of books together. Some of them I carried home and others I read to the boys right on the spot. Every now and then as I read through the pages, I thought, *I could have written that book.* Or, *I could have told a better story that this one.*

If you've said this statement (or even thought about saying it), keep reading because I want to give you some insight about the children's book market. Many authors will go to their computers, open a blank file and write a story, then go to a market guide and fire that manuscript off to a publisher and earn their first rejection form letter. While their enthusiasm for the children's book market is admirable, these writers have violated one of the first principles to getting published: *They have not studied the market.*

Until I worked inside a company that published children's books, I never understood the huge expense related to producing simple

24-page or 32-page full-color books. While the advances for these books to the writer are often in the modest $1,000 to $2,000 range, the actual cost can easily reach over $100,000. You can see how the decision to publish a children's book is not made lightly—at least if the publisher wants to remain in business.

Notice in the previous paragraph that I mentioned 24-page and 32-pages. Children's picture books have a standard length. This detail is important to understand about the market if you want to write for children. If you propose a book which is not formatted or pitched in the standard format, you are practically begging to be rejected for your lack of study. If you understand the current children's book marketplace, then this understanding will show in your submission and your work will stand out from the other books submitted to a children's book editor.

I've Written Children's Books

Although the bulk of my work over the last 20 years has been in adult books, I've also published a number of children's books with traditional publishers. I've written everything from full-color simple stories targeted for three to five year olds to 32-page books for four to seven year olds. I've also written more than half a dozen biographies targeted to 8-to-12-year-old readers.

Why biographies? I have always been fascinated by stories about other people. The summers of my youth were often spent living several months with my granny in Frankfort, Kentucky. I made frequent trips to the local library and carried home stacks of books about various leaders throughout American history and others. With this background, I was a natural to write stories about other people and a variety of youth biographies.

While I wanted to write books in the early days of my writing, I did not jump immediately into books. I honed my writing craft in magazine articles and other shorter forms of writing. I learned to write a query letter to pitch my idea and then when I got an assignment, I wrote the article and sent it in to the publication. Throughout those early years of my writing, I was building a reputation for excellence in the magazine area and learning about books through writing book reviews. I was the original book review columnist for *Christian Parenting Today* (which went out of business years ago but originally had a circulation of about 150,000 readers). I also reviewed books for a number of other publications, and I read a broad sweep of children's books and teen books—fiction and nonfiction.

In general, writers do not get much pay for writing book reviews, but you do receive free review copies of books from the publishers. I read and considered many more books than the ones I ended up writing about for the various publications. At that time, several publishers added my name to their list of media who received review copies of all of their new releases. It amounted to hundreds of children's books coming to my mailbox and in the process of reading that material, taught me a great deal about the marketplace.

Besides reading children's books and writing magazine articles, I also started to attend writer's conferences and meet book editors. One of those conversations gave me the opportunity to write my first book—a children's book.

While talking with the editor during a writer's conference, she said to me, "Terry, as a part of our company mission statement, we are to challenge children with the needs of the world. Yet in our full array of children's books, we don't have a single book that addresses this issue. What types of ideas do you have?"

I had never thought about this question before but unknowingly, through my writing and reading, I had been preparing an answer. At the time, Lion Books had a popular series of children's books from author Stephen Lawhead which combined real pictures with a cartoon character. This imaginative series evolved around a character named Howard and the books included: *Howard Had a Hot Air Balloon* and *Howard Had a Space Ship*.

After thinking for a few minutes, I suggested, "What if we combined pictures from around the world with a cartoon character to show children they could grow up and go anywhere in the world?"

Instantly the editor resonated with the idea and she said, "That's a good idea, Terry. Please write that up and send it to me." I made a little notation about my concept and in the subsequent weeks I wrote a manuscript and sent it to the editor. We went through a number of versions of the manuscript but eventually that same editor offered me a book contract—my first. In 1992, a hardcover full-color book for children ages 4 to 7 was released. It combined real photographs from around the world with a cartoon character who moved into different occupations and was called, *When I Grow Up, I Can Go Anywhere for Jesus*. This title marked my entrance into the world of book publishing.

Hope for the Future

The children's inspirational market has become much more competitive over the last several years. There are fewer publishers and they are being much more selective. One of the things I never understood as a children's author, until I worked for a publisher, is the huge amount of money required to produce a full-color children's book. It's because the artwork is generally purchased in full with all rights from the artist to the publisher, and that raises the expense but also the risk for the publisher who has to recover this type of investment. It's a high-dollar business and not something to be done lightly.

Many writers look at the children's market as simple, and these books as easy to write with only a few words. But the publisher looks at a lot of poorly crafted manuscripts to find the ones they eventually publish. Some of the inspirational publishers have given up in the children's area. Concordia has cut back in the children's book area. There are still publishers like Nelson, Tyndale, Zondervan, Bethany House, Standard, Cook, and others who continue to make strides in this area, but the competition is stiff. There is also competition between the new books and the backlist, or older books, which continue to sell. Many of these backlist titles are bestsellers which publishers keep in print, in stock, and in the bookstores for many years. Writers do well to craft their manuscripts, study the market, and form relationships with editors at writer's conferences and persevere in their work.

When I was a literary agent, almost every week I received queries from would-be children's writers asking me to represent their work. These requests continued in spite of the clear message in the agency guidelines that I was not interested in representing children's books.

Many writers have no idea of the reasons few literary agents represent children's writers. These would-be authors never consider business realities the agents face. First, I've mentioned the high financial cost and risk for the publishers. Children's writers believe because there are few words on the page, that the expense would be small for a children's book. The publishers who are successful make careful decisions about what they print—and even then, they are often surprised. I recall a specific series of children's books where one of my former publishers put a large amount of money and energy into marketing and producing full-color, graded picture books. These books entered the marketplace with great fanfare—but in a few short years have faded from the marketplace. When I was writing this section, I did a search and found used copies, but nothing on the publisher site. This indicates these books are out of print at a huge loss for the publisher. Authors don't think about this risk when they propose their little children's book idea to a publisher or literary agent.

Second, many children's advances are modest. Literary agents work on commission or a percentage of the deal (typically 15 percent). Now, take off your writer's hat for a minute and look at your children's submission from the agent's view. Understanding the average first-time children's author with a traditional publisher may receive a $500 or $1,000 advance for their book—and that 90 percent of nonfiction books never earn back that advance or additional funds— which would you want to be selling as an agent? Would you rather sell an adult novel, a nonfiction book proposal for a larger advance (even for a first-time author) or a children's book? Simple economics are one of the reasons that it's hard for a children's writer to find a literary agent to represent their work.

Third, book packagers produce many children's books. Publishers are looking for ways to reduce the production costs on a book, have less people on their staff, and still produce a number of products to sell into the marketplace. One of the methods many of them use is a book packager who produces the book under the supervision of someone inside the publishing house. These packagers hire the writer and designer and then give the production files to the publisher for printing. If you want to write these types of books, then you need to be approaching the packager for an assignment. One of the best ways to learn about this part of the business is through the American Book Producer Association and their Web site (www.abpaonline.org).

Look around their site and contact some of their members. Packagers hire the writer for a flat fee or under a "work-made-for-hire" agreement. It is a good way to break into the children's market and have some published books.

You may be wondering, "Where is the hope for the future of children's publishing?" One of the first steps for a writer is to face the realities of the marketplace. With this understanding you will increase your chances for success.

I recommend that you purchase current book market and magazine market guides from the Institute of Children's Literature. The information in these annual guides changes constantly but will stir many ideas about how you can enter various parts of the children's market. If you prepare your material professionally and study the marketplace, your excellence will shine through in the submission process.

Many children's writers have tunnel vision. They only want to write children's books, yet they first need to build their visibility and reputation in the magazine market. Writing for children is a noble and good idea—but you have to be armed with good information or you will simply collect rejections.

Principles to Help Any Writer

While the children's market is highly competitive, the editors and publishers in this area continue to search for quality writers. There are opportunities for you to be published but as this chapter draws to a close, let me draw several principles to help your efforts. Even if you are not a children's writer, you can use these same principles to write in your particular niche.

Once a month she purified the mailbox of the Evil Spirit of Rejection.

1. **Get acquainted with the various nuances of the children's market.** The books are targeted for specific age categories and you should become familiar with these ranges. You need to have a specific target market for your book manuscript. The vocabulary and topics will be different for each age group and your manuscript will have a better reception if you understand these rules. At the end of this chapter, I include a number of resources to help you with this information.

2. **Be flexible in your goals and dreams**. Show your talent by writing for children's magazines or the education marketplace. Be flexible and willing to take any opportunity. For example, many writers are looking only for a royalty arrangement, but many children's publishers only offer the writer a "work-made-

for-hire" agreement or a flat fee. Are you willing to write under these conditions? I have written a number of books under a work-made-for-hire agreement.

3. **Join children's organizations.** One of the best for children's writers is the Society of Children's Book Writers and Illustrators. You don't have to be published to become a member, and they have an extensive array of resources and aids to teach you more about the children's marketplace.

4. **Take training** such as courses from the Institute of Children's Literature. The ICL has been training writers for many years. I love their course materials and their style of instruction. For over two years, I taught at the ICL and mentored many students through the process of writing children's books. As an instructor, I critiqued the lessons and returned them to the students, encouraging them to move ahead with their dreams, and a plan for children's writing.

5. **Continue to build your relationships** with editors and explore their needs. Can you write to one of their needs? Many writers are focused only on writing what they want to write. In general these writers ignore the marketplace and the needs of an editor. In the process, they are missing many opportunities for their children's writing to be published and to hone their craft.

6. **Be persistent** and keep working at it. You never know where you will find the open door for your next opportunity to write a children's book. Are you open to new possibilities?

The Magical Experience

"Grandpa Terry, will you read to me?" It was a small voice that I could not refuse. I chose a children's book from my shelf and curled up in a chair with the small child on my lap. For a few minutes, we whirled into another world. From time to time, we would stop and talk about the illustrations or the story, and then continue until we reached the final page.

As I closed the book I was thankful for the opportunity to have written such a story years earlier. The majority of my children's books are out of print but I still have a few copies which I have saved for special occasions and magical experiences.

Dig Deeper

1. *How To Publish Your Children's Book* by Lisa N. Burby (SquareOne Publishers, 2004). This award-winning author of 38 nonfiction, history, science, health, and social issue books has pulled together a comprehensive book about children's writing. Subtitled "How to Maximize Your Odds of Getting Your work Into Print," I'm impressed with the depth and scope of this book.

2. Another book to consider is the annual *Children's Writer Guide to _specific year___* edited by Susan Tierney. The Writer's Bookstore. 95 Long Ridge Rd., West Redding, CT 06896, or 1-800-443-6078, or www.WritersBookstorecom. This annual guide is loaded with information about the market, research, writing tips, and trends.

3. *The Giblin Guide to Writing Children's Books* by James Cross Giblin. 2005 The Writer's Bookstore. 95 Long Ridge Rd., West Redding, CT 06896, 1-800-443-6078, or www.WritersBookstore.com. For 30 years, Jim Giblin has been a children's book editor and publisher, and during the last 22 years, he's been the editor-in-chief at Clarion Books. This fourth edition is a classic and loaded with sound advice for children's authors from a skilled expert.

4. *How to Write and Sell Children's Picture Books* by Jean E. Karl (Writer's Digest Books, 1994). This author worked on the classic Dick and Jane books as well as founding the children's department at Atheneum Publishers. As an insider, she instructs how to select the right type of children's book (fiction, nonfiction, poetry, or novelty), how to write each of these types of books, marketing, and promotion.

Awaken Your Dreams

1. Write a series of ideas that you would like to publish in the children's book area. Are they fiction or nonfiction? Do you have a specific targeted age group?

2. Plan a course of action to write these manuscripts and then get them into the marketplace.

CHAPTER 18

Repurpose Your Content

After reading the previous 17 chapters in *Jumpstart Your Publishing Dreams*, it is natural to feel overwhelmed. While at first it looks simple to get into the publishing world, you will be much more successful with a bit of planning and purpose behind your work.

What if you could increase the effectiveness and earning power of the material you are creating? If you would like to learn easier ways to create products, then you need the details in this chapter on how to repurpose your material. I believe the concepts could revolutionize the way you achieve your publishing dreams.

Most people outside of the publishing community assume they will make money writing books, but the publishing numbers present a different story. More than 90 percent of nonfiction books never earn back their advance. Within traditional publishing, you don't pay someone else to publish your book (self-publishing) but instead, the publisher pays you an advance as a part of the contract. For many first-time authors, this advance is modest ($5,000 to $10,000). An advance is just what it means—an advance against royalties or earnings of the book. If you flip the statistic, only 10 percent of books from traditional publishers earn additional money over and above the advance. Now consider these sales numbers for books. In 2004, about 1.2 million books were in print. Eighty percent of those books sold fewer than 100 copies and 98 percent sold fewer than 5,000 copies.

I've probably done some serious bursting of your dreams about earning wealth from getting a book published. Keep reading, however, because I have good news for you in the pages that follow but it will involve a drastic revision of your expectations related to publishing.

Internet marketing expert, Alex Mandossian, has conducted over 23,000 teleseminars with best-selling authors. In fact, Alex created the virtual book tour so authors can sell their books quicker, faster, and with less human effort. From his observation of many authors, Alex says, "Authors don't make money writing books; they make money (monetize) *explaining* books."

In the fall of 2002, north of San Francisco, Mandossian was meeting a friend for dinner in Corte Madera. The parking lot was packed and he had to park several blocks away. Mandossian noticed people rushing past him carrying hardcover books and streaming into a bookstore called Book Passage. "Who is signing books?" he wondered.

The crowd had gathered because Al Gore—who two years earlier had just left the vice presidency—and his wife Tipper were signing copies of a book called *Joined At the Heart: The Transformation of the American Family* (Holt Paperback). At a 15 or 20 percent royalty, Mandossian wondered how many books sold at such a packed author signing. After dinner, he went to the bookstore and the crowd had dispersed. He asked the sales person, "How many books did you sell?"

"Over 400 books," the woman glowed. "It's the most successful book signing we've ever had." In general, this signing was successful because, on average, an author will sell few books at such a physical signing. *Chicken Soup for the Soul* authors, Jack Canfield and Mark Victor Hansen, have told Mandossian about book signings where no one purchased a single book. He could see why the retailer was excited about selling 400 books in a single evening.

Mandossian saw the irony of such a signing. The former vice president has been traveling constantly for the last eight years and only sells 400 books in an evening. In that moment, Mandossian had the idea to create a virtual book tour where authors could invite readers to a teleseminar event to talk about the contents of their books and sell books.

According to Mandossian, authors make money on their books through explaining it to potential readers and talking about their book. Yet he measured those sales against the wear and tear of traveling around the nation meeting people face-to-face in bookstores. Because Mandossian teaches a course called Teleseminar Secrets, he decided to niche his course for authors and literary agents which would give authors a way to approach a large audience with their book.

In collaboration with Paul Colligan, Mandossian published *The Business Podcasting Bible* (www.thebusinesspodcastingbible.com) which sells for $19.95. Instead of laboring to craft the words and write the book, Colligan and Mandossian repurposed their audio teaching into this book. First, the pair taught a $1,300 six-part class called *Podcasting Secrets*. Their teleseminar teaching is loaded with detailed how-to information. The audio content was transcribed using a system like www.idictate.com. Next the material was edited into a book manuscript which was self-published and available through Amazon and other online stores. Why would they go to the effort to produce a printed book? Because the book gives them another venue for their content, with no extra effort, plus it serves as a substantial business card to promote their online business.

If you are a speaker or teacher on a particular topic, can you follow some of the same steps to repurpose your content into a book or a set of audio CDs combined with a notebook that you can sell? It is a matter of understanding the value of repurposing your content and understanding that publishing is more than writing for magazines or writing books. It can also be producing a series of audios, a course in a three-ring binder, a series of teleseminars, or an audio coaching e-course or ????. The only limitations are your own creativity.

The idea of repurposing has been around for years. About 15 years ago, I attended a workshop at a writer's conference on the topic of selling reprints. While I can't recall the specific author, she was a master at reselling her magazine work. At any given time, this author had about 1,000 of her reprints in circulation to various publications. In magazine publishing, you usually sell only the first North American rights to a publication. After your article is printed in that magazine, the rights return to you as the author. Many smaller publications will take reprints and you can resell the same article as a reprint to them. This author developed a system that whenever one of her magazine articles was published, she began to market it to other publications as a reprint. When a submission came back rejected, she sent it to another magazine and got it into the consideration process. Her efforts were adding to her earnings for each article, as well as the exposure of her work in the marketplace.

At the time, I was writing for a number of magazines. After going to this workshop, I tried to remarket reprints and did place a number of them, receiving additional income from that work. Yet in general,

I found it difficult to keep up with the ever-changing magazine markets, and also found that often the reprints are paid at a much lower rate than original material. I chalked my work on reprints up to a learning experience and returned to creating more original content for a magazine or a book publisher. At the time, I didn't understand the power or value of repurposed content.

For the past several years, I've been traveling around the United States and Canada teaching at various writers' conferences. Usually, my workshops are recorded and I receive a complimentary copy of the CD presentation. I pick up my copy, tuck it into my carry-on luggage, and bring it home. When I unpack, I throw the audio into my desk drawer where it is not replayed and does absolute zero good for anyone (including me). I have compiled a wealth of material which can be repurposed, published to help others, and make increased income.

Several years ago, I attended Mega Book Marketing University 2007 and heard the CD presentations from the speakers. Each of these presentations begins and ends with the same jazzy little tune. From the instant you turn on the program, the music begins and it mentally prepares you for the next speaker. These CDs are branded or connected through the music which is called "needle music" and is royalty-free. Online you can easily find different vendors for royalty-free music.

I purchased a simple-to-use program called Sound Forge (www.autopilotriches.com/app/?af=556435). This menu-driven program allows you to edit sound in the same way Microsoft Word allows you to edit text. In a relatively short amount of time, I added short segments of the same music to the beginning and end of several related workshops and put them into a teaching package called *Editor Reveals Book Proposal Secrets* (www.editorbookproposals.com).

On the surface, it may look like I have a large warehouse of these products. I don't. I'm using Speaker Fulfillment (www.speakerfulfillmentservices.com) which allows you to make a small quantity of the recordings. I've built a single page Web site called a micro-site to sell the product, and use a shopping cart called www.mywebmarketingmagic.com. The shopping cart calculates the shipping and postage when someone purchases the CD set. Speaker Fulfillment Services fills the order and ships the product. It is another way to repurpose content.

While this type of system works well for several recordings to be collected into a single product, what if you have many hours of audio material that you want to repurpose into an audio product? I suggest you look into www.myseminarplayer.com where you can create custom portable media players to use in your repurposing efforts.

Use Teleseminars to Repurpose Content

I've taught many writers about book proposal creation. Teleseminars can be a way you can create content and then repurpose that content. For my teleseminars, I used the tool: www.myinstanttelewebcast.com. Use this tool to record your sessions and then download the recording. During a teleseminar about book proposal creation, I received over 270 questions from writers. Some of the questions were duplicated and others were unique. I organized them into the top 50 questions about book proposal creation, and then repurposed these questions into an audio coaching program called Proposal Secrets (www.proposalsecrets.com).

If you take the Proposal Secrets course, you will receive a daily audio postcard for 50 consecutive days. If you learn best as an audio learner, you will hear a frequently asked question about book proposal creation—and my answer. If it is better for your style of learning to read and study a printed version of the question, then each question includes a PDF downloadable transcript.

Marketing to Repurpose Your Content

Several years ago Amazon, the largest online bookstore on the planet, launched a program called Amazon Shorts. You could submit writing between 2,000 to 10,000 words which Amazon formatted and sold as digital downloads for $.49. I created a marketing/teaching article called *Straight Talk from the Editor, 18 Keys to a Rejection-Proof Submission.* For the first six months of the release, Amazon had an exclusive arrangement by which they were the only ones who could sell the product. I learned Amazon had permission to sell only the digital products within the United States, and overseas writers who wanted access would contact me. Also Amazon collected all of the customer information and paid me 50 percent of the income from the sales.

After the six-month period, I took the content of this publication and repurposed it into a new product which you can get at: www.straighttalkeditor.com. Because I controlled the content, I am able to edit it, update it, and also use it as a personal marketing tool. It is another idea for you to consider for repurposing your content.

Writing on Purpose

Over a period of several years, Dr. Dennis Hensley wrote a series of magazine articles on related topics which were published. Dr. Hensley wanted to repurpose this material so he put the articles into a cohesive book idea and created a book proposal. Then he marketed the book proposal and got a publisher.

In order to repurpose your magazine writing into a book, you have to be conscious of several factors. First, the material while created separately has to be written into a single project with a central theme. Second, remember the material had to be well-written in the first place to have been published in various magazines. If you strategically write in a certain niche or area of the market, you could follow this pattern to repurpose your writing and get more exposure and payment for it.

A Series of Repurposing Ideas

While this chapter has presented a series of possibilities, there are many other ways to repurpose your material and jumpstart your publishing.

In chapter 13, I discussed the importance of building an online presence and starting an online newsletter. Have you created a blog which is focused on a particular topic? Can you take this blog material and repurpose it into individual articles? If so, you can use these articles in your own newsletter or market them into services, like ezinearticles.com, where others can also use them. Through these types of services you can gain much more use for your writing through repurposing.

Consider the Blook

Several years ago, the word "blog"—which is short for web log— entered the English language. There are millions of blogs. Some of them have gained large followings and the authors have repurposed their blog material into books—which are called a "blook."

For a year, Julie Powell blogged about her experiences of executing the recipes of Julia Child's *Mastering the Art of French Cooking*. She repurposed this material from her blog into *Julie and Julia: 365 Days, 524 Recipes, 1 Tiny Apartment Kitchen* (Little & Brown, 2005) which sold over 100,000 copies.

There are a number of writers who have successfully taken their blog material and repurposed it into a blook or a best-selling printed book.

Planning and forethought are key elements in repurposing your content. Sometimes you are focused only on one product and don't take into consideration the entire realm of possibilities. For example, you are focused on getting your book published and a publisher believes in your idea and offers you a contract (yeah!). The book contract from the publisher is sweeping and takes almost any possible rights for future publication. If you have other plans for that material, you can attempt to negotiate and keep some of those rights. For example, the publisher doesn't have any activity with their current books in the electronic realm or Ebook. Can you keep those electronic rights or give them the "nonexclusive" rights? If so, you've given yourself some room to repurpose your content and gain more mileage from your writing. If you have some out-of-print books, it's possible but often difficult to resell that book to another publisher. You can repurpose your material into an Ebook and get much more traction with it.

I'd encourage you to get the broadest possible use of your writing through repurposing. It will earn you increased income and greater use from the effort of your writing.

Dig Deeper

1. 1. If you would like to learn more about Teleseminar Secrets for Authors, go to www.telseminarsecret.com and you can download a teleseminar that I did with D'vorah Lansky who teaches authors how to use this technology.

2. Download *Straight Talk from the Editor* (www.straighttalkeditor. com) and study it to see how I put it together. Can you learn something about repurposing your own content as you study how I've repurposed mine?

3. Learn more about teleseminars and how this tool is used to repurpose content and promote books. Go to: www. alexmandossian.com/category/virtual-book-tours, listen to several of Alex Mandossian's Virtual Book Tours and watch his technique and learn from it.

Awaken Your Dreams

1. Have you been producing content for years such as magazine articles or a blog? Plan a course of action so you can repurpose that material into a different product. Plan your own strategy to get it into the marketplace.

2. Is there some skill that you write about or teach about on a regular basis? I encourage you to look into launching your own online course like I did about book proposal creation. Consider purchasing the Simple Membership System at: www.yourmembershipcourse.com.

CHAPTER 19

Engage the Marketplace

Kevin dreamed about writing and getting some of his work into print. While he naturally thought about that printed work in a book format, he also was willing to learn about magazines. At the library, he checked out a book, read it and located a couple of potential markets. Then he sent his material to the publisher and waited. In a matter of only a few weeks, he received form rejections from both places and decided that writing wasn't for him. He tucked his book manuscript away in a file and turned to other things.

On the other side of the country, Bill loved to write books and even had a contract with a major publisher. Yet he was months late on meeting his deadline. He was not apologetic about because he knew writers are often late on their deadlines. Each time Bill spoke with his editor about an extension, she noticed that Bill managed to notify his large Twitter audience about the blow-by-blow details of his day and also blogged several times a day. While Bill's social marketing skills were admirable, he continued to delay his obligation to his publisher.

These two men have approached the issue of marketing from polar opposite perspectives. Kevin doesn't want to have anything to do with marketing or selling or getting his work out to editors or the public. He loves to write but hates to do anything about "marketing." In sharp contrast, Bill grabs on to anything new in the marketing area and spends hours on it to learn all of the nuances of it, but doesn't meet his writing deadlines.

People love to talk about their books and how they wrote something—but they don't love the actual writing process. Why? For many individuals, the actual writing is hard work. Clear communication and crafting the stories into words on the page take a lot of effort.

The publishing marketplace is in constant motion. For example, the Internet figures much more prominently into the plans of authors and publishers than it was even a few years ago. The majority of people in the U.S. have high speed Internet connections and it leads to a growing use of video for teaching and book promotion. It seems like almost monthly some brand new marketing concept springs on the scene.

How do you determine which new marketing concepts to embrace and which to ignore? Each person only has a limited amount of writing time and a limited amount of time to give to marketing. Where do you find the balance?

Nine Basic Principles

There are many more ways to connect with the market than I can cover in this chapter. But through my years of working in publishing, these nine principles play a key role in ways I engage the marketplace.

1. Always be prepared to leave behind some connection to yourself and your work. You should follow the motto of the Boy Scouts, "Be Prepared." Every time I get into my car to drive, I carry my driver's license. It's a long-term habit. Develop the marketing habit of preparation so you are always ready with a business card or a copy of your latest book. Why include a book? You may discover someone of influence where it is perfect to give that book away so the person will read it and talk about it to others.

When I travel, sometimes I engage the person beside me in conversation. Recently on a plane trip, I mentioned my role as an acquisitions editor. The person next to me said, "My friend in Australia is writing a novel and she is looking for a publisher. Do you have a business card?"

When I ask someone for their business card, often people will dig into their wallet or purse and rummage around for several minutes to see if they have the information. Instead, I'm ready for the question and carry several business cards in my shirt pocket within easy reach. I handed her my business card. Several weeks after this exchange, I received an email from Australia and the writer mentioned her friend sat beside me on a flight to Ohio. She wanted to know if I was interested in her novel. I've exchanged several emails with this novelist. The conversation was initiated because I was prepared to give my business card to a new person. On many occasions, I've given a business card or a bookmark or a postcard. If you create such marketing tools as business cards, postcards and bookmarks and carry them with you, then you can be prepared to engage the market. You never know where the door will lead if you aren't prepared to walk through it.

2. Decide to be consistent. Marketing yourself or your book is not a one-time effort. An old marketing adage is the Rule of Seven. It says that a potential buyer has to hear your marketing message at least seven times before they take action. While this number isn't cast in stone, behind the Rule of Seven is the truth that you can't tell someone once or twice and expect to sell your book. An example would be starting a blog, and then consistently adding to that blog on a regular basis. Many blogs do not have readers because people don't know the blog exists. One simple method to market your blog or website to others is to write a simple tag for the blog then add it to your email signature line. For example, my blog is called The Writing Life: www.thewritinglife.ws. If you use it in your emails on a consistent basis, people will follow the link and learn about your blog. Besides telling people about your blog, you will need to write content which attracts people and they want to read on a regular basis.

3. Decide to be generous and others will reciprocate. Each individual has gained information and insight that we learn which we can pass along to others. Maybe you pass it along on a blog or through an online group or through an electronic newsletter. It may feel like you are giving without any return but I believe that type of giving is attractive and will be paid back to you. For example, each book sold on Amazon has a place for customer reviews. These reviews are recommended to be 75 to 300 words and do not require a long time to write. One of the simple ways through the years that I've supported good books is to write a review of that book on Amazon. Many times a book only has a few book reviews and you can influence others to purchase that book. When I buy a book on Amazon, I will often look at the various customer reviews to see what people are saying about it. If you write positive reviews about the books which you have read, you will likely be one of the few people to write about that book—and you can tell the author about your review. I've written over 400 customer reviews of books on Amazon. While I'm not paid for these reviews, it is a way that I'm generous with others and it builds goodwill. It's rare that I ask someone else for help but I believe because of my generosity with others, they are often open to helping me.

4. Count the cost for each new marketing tool. Consider the consequences in terms of time and what else needs to be eliminated from your life. Will you have to cut back on your reading or your time watching television or involvement with your family or what? To add something will require that you cut elsewhere. With this principle, the key is to consider the cost and then make a careful decision.

5. Gain knowledge before starting a new area of the market. There is an old saying, "Look before you leap." Often writers will jump into a new technology without a plan or a clue and make some basic gaffs which could have been easily prevented with some orientation. For example, millions of people have joined the social marketing area such as Facebook or Twitter. Others begin a blog without selecting a topic to write something interesting. Others simply forget everyone can read whatever you post to the Internet. You gain this knowledge in several ways. First, take the time to observe how others are using the particular marketing strategy. Can you imitate their methods or improve on them? Second, use Google and search for some free Ebooks to give you some information and background on the marketing strategy. If you type these words into Google: "Facebook Free Ebook," you will discover several possible Ebooks to avoid some common mistakes. Millions of people are using Twitter without a plan or some basic orientation. Get my free Ebook, Mastering Twitter in 10 Minutes or Less at: www.terrylinks.com/MT. Alex Mandossian often says, "Always improve and never invent," a statement packed with wisdom.

6. Look for ways to automate. Often there are free or inexpensive tools which can help you be more effective with your marketing efforts. I encourage you to keep a constant watch for such tools and then incorporate them into your routine.

On a regular basis during the last year, individuals will email me or tell me in person how much they appreciate the publishing information which I put on Facebook. The first time I received this compliment, I said thank you yet inside I was wondering, "How am I active on Facebook? I rarely visit this website." Each day (at least when I'm not traveling), I send out several tweets on Twitter. My tweets are focused on the area of writing or publishing. Then I remembered how the same information appears on Facebook. Some time ago, I found a free application on Facebook which automatically duplicates my tweets without any action on my part. Be aware that you can use such tools and gain greater marketing exposure with little or no additional effort. Writers are some of the best procrastinators. Often I overhear writers say they spent hours reading posts on Twitter or Facebook. Instead I read a few people and ignore the masses so I can get some other key things accomplished. You can make the same types of choices for your marketing.

7. Be open to new tools. You will discover these new tools in many different ways such as in a blog post or in an email. Also, if you are using something like Twitter or Facebook check out the different applications, which are available for these marketing tools. For example, with Twitter, one of the tools I regularly use is called Hootsuite (www.hootsuite.com). It's free and allows me to quickly create short links to any additional information. When the person clicks on a hootsuite link, it will open a new window with a toolbar across the top. Then someone can "retweet" or pass on the link to others. Through using it, you have made it easy for others to pass on your information and continue your marketing efforts. The only reason I learned about hootsuite is my own willingness to try new tools. Or if you have a book to promote, I encourage you to go to John Kremer's massive website, www.bookmarket.com and look around at his extensive content. Follow the links and learn from his expertise. I've only given two of countless new tools available to help your marketing efforts. These tools will help your marketing efforts only if you are open to using them.

8. Don't neglect printed tools such as bookmarks or postcards or business cards. While much of the marketing efforts are focused on the Internet, there is continued value in some of the "tried and true" methods of direct mail. These printed tools can be a powerful method to reach people who will never see you online.

At the same time, put thought, energy and planning into the creation of these tools. Whether it is a postcard, a business card or a bookmark you have a small space to interest your reader then provide some critical information. Often I have received these tools and they are missing critical information such as the price of the book or the ISBN (International Standard Book Number or the reference point for any book). If you are speaking in person to audiences, create a bookmark to leave behind—whether they purchase your book or not. While bookmarks may appear simple, consider carefully what information you put on the bookmark. When you only have a few words, you need to select the right information such as a short quotation, the price of your book, the publisher, the ISBN and where they can purchase the book. To some, postcards are known as "naked mail" because studies show many people read a postcard as it goes through the mail system.

The prices for these direct mail tools can vary. Use a search engine like Google then search for a term like "print postcards" to locate potential vendors. Many companies will offer to mail you some free samples of their products. Ask for these samples before you order to ensure they are producing a high quality product and you will like the results. Also ask your friends for a recommendation and then actively use these "direct-to-reader" tools.

9. Create a clear goal for each marketing tool. When you learn about a new marketing tool, you are not just using it to use it. In addition, you need to have a goal in mind. In each case, it's good to have a stated goal for each effort. For example, if you are going to print 1,000 postcards to promote your book. You can make a plan to use them within six months of printing—either through mailing them or face to face promotion. Without a goal, you are just as likely to stick them in your desk drawer and they never reach the intended individuals. Postcard promotion helps in your larger goal of exposing more people to your book.

Make sure each tool helps you move toward your larger goals. If the tool isn't helping you reach your larger goals then it is a distraction and something to eliminate. You can expect to have a learning curve with any new tool but after a period of time, it's good to evaluate each tool and see if it is moving you toward your larger publishing goals.

If you follow these nine principles, they will increase your effectiveness as you engage the ever-changing marketplace. You will learn to use new these new tools to grow your audience and readers. In the next few pages of this chapter, I will provide a 30,000 foot level perspective of several marketing tools and how they can help you reach your goals for publishing.

"We're going 'online'. You've got
24 hours to figure out the 'web'
and explain it to me."

Blogs

Technorati is the recognized authority to track over 112.8 million blogs or "weblogs." This number does not include all the 72.82 million Chinese blogs which The China Internet Network Information Center tracks. While these blog statistics often concern the English language blogosphere, don't forget about the millions of blogs in other languages that are not always included in estimations.[22]

You may have considered blogging as a private journal but I suggest blogging is a valuable tool to use with your publishing efforts. Since late 2004, I've been writing about publishing and writing in a blog called The Writing Life (www.thewritinglife.ws). At this writing, I have over 1,200 searchable entries and volumes of material with at least 500 readers a day. I know the number of readers because a free tool called sitemeter (www.sitemeter.com) measures the visitors each day. In addition, over 500 people receive each of my updates in their email box through another free tool, Feedblitz (www.feedblitz.com).

Make sure you create a distinct look for your blog. If you start a blog on your topic like The Writing Life, you will increase your presence online. The search engines like blogs because they contain new content. Also before you start writing a blog, I encourage you to take the necessary time to read several blogs in your topic area. Notice the writing style of the blogger and the types of things they include in your blog. As you read these blogs, you will begin to understand the type of material which you want to include and recognize other entries which you don't want to include in your blog.

Before you launch your blog, make sure you are writing about a topic where you have a great deal of passion and enthusiasm. Also select a topic which is broad enough to have many types of entries. Some planning time before you launch a blog will help you grow your audience and sustain your entries over the long haul. People will return to read your new entries because they expect to learn more about your topic. For example, I write about matters related to publishing and writing. It is harder to grow an audience if you bounce from one subject area to another.

Because of tools like Google Alerts, you need to understand a blog is not private but a public forum of communication. In my blog, I quoted journalists who have written for publications like The New Yorker. Within 48 hours, I received a personal email from that journalist. I encourage you to treat the writing in your blog as though you are publishing another issue of a printed magazine. It helps you to keep in mind that your entries have a broad potential readership. Because my entries are captured in the search engines, at times someone will comment about a blog entry which I wrote several years ago. Anyone can comment on my blog but each comment is delivered into my mailbox. Sometimes these comments are from spammers so it's a good idea to monitor them—and have the ability to quickly delete something which is irrelevant from your blog.

Some blogs contain one or two entries and no one reads them. How do you attract a growing audience of readers? Bloggers prefer each site to have a distinct look so I worked with a designer to create a unique look for these entries. I've also added tools like Feedblitz and a free search tool from Google to increase the usefulness of it. Frequency is important for blogs and growing your readers so I make a point of blogging several times a week. If I'm traveling or away from my computer where it's hard to blog, I "announce" my plans on the blog so readers will know what is happening. Otherwise some of my readers will write me and ask about it. Also I include a link to my blog in most of my email signature lines (the place at the bottom where you identify yourself). These signature lines remind people about my entries and increase my readers. Besides consistency another key for blogging is to pick a topic and stick with it.

Whether you are blogging or using another marketing tool, always look for free or inexpensive add-ons which will either help give you more exposure or allow you to be flexible in the writing process. For example, I use a program called Blog Jet to write my entries offline and save them on my computer. Also I use an inexpensive program called Blog Blaster. With a single button, Blog Blaster notifies or "pings" a large number of blog search engines that I have added a new entry to my blog. New tools are being constantly developed in this ever-changing environment and my encouragement is to be aware of them and use them. You can easily locate these tools and others such as Google Alerts through a search engine like Google.

Online Groups

Thousands of online groups have been organized around any possible topic. You can locate some of them on Yahoo in the Groups section. Some of these groups only have a few members while others have thousands of members. The majority of these groups are free and you can learn from their expertise and gain exposure for yourself and your own publishing success. Let me give you several cautions. You can waste hours reading frivolous messages and participating in these groups when you could be writing or other tasks related to your publishing dreams. Yet you can also gain readers and increase your audience through your participation. Like other marketing efforts, the key is balance and planning. I encourage you to join several of them and take a period of time to catch the dynamics of the group. These online groups frown on people who jump right into their discussions only to promote a product or themselves. Instead participate in the discussions with a link to your writing in your signature line or where you provide your name.

I'm actively involved in several of these online groups because it reminds people about my writing and services. These groups of friends celebrate your achievements and sympathize with your struggles. In these groups, you can make lasting friendships which will help you accomplish your publishing dreams.

LinkedIn

When I first received an invitation to a site called LinkedIn, I deleted them because I could not see the value. As of this writing, LinkedIn is an online network of more than 60 million experienced professionals from more than 200 countries, representing 150 industries. Using the free services of this site, I have started and maintained some valuable relationships within the publishing community. Like the other tools in this chapter, LinkedIn is not a magic bullet to solve all of your issues related to maintaining your connections. I've found it useful and if you go to my public profile at: www.linkedin.com/in/terrywhalin, you will notice that I have the maximum of more than 500 connections. LinkedIn is a good place to display your professional background and credentials to other professionals.

Other Social Networks

In these pages, I've only scratched the surface of the social network phenomena. Millions of people have started to Twitter. On this site, you have 140 characters to answer the question, "What are you doing now?" As I've suggested with other sites, look for people who are successful and see how they are using the system, then follow their example. For example one of the early adopters of Twitter was Guy Kawasaki, a Silicon Valley venture capitalist. At the time of this writing, Kawasaki has over 1,395,000 people "following" him on Twitter. Each time Kawasaki sends out a Twitter update, he reaches these followers on their cell phones or computers with information about him or an interesting article or product. As with the other tools in this chapter, look for tools to help you use Twitter without wasting time. Beyond Twitter, others are using Facebook, MySpace and Ning along with many other social network systems to promote their business or writing or publishing efforts. Each person must make careful decisions about each of these tools. Many writers are procrastinators and some of these social marketing tools will fuel your tendency in this area. Writers will tell me that they have spent all morning reading their Facebook or Twitter feed instead of writing. It is important to use the different principles and evaluate each tool in light of your goals and purpose *before* you realize you've lost valuable time because of some social networking tool.

Do Book Reviews Matter?

The Sunday edition of the Arizona Republic Newspaper has a circulation of over 500,000 copies. Each week in the Arts and Entertainment section, they review **four books**. I normally read these reviews because I'm interested in seeing which four books are selected each week.

Recently the Republic reviewed a new thriller, *Final Target*, from a first-time author, Steven Gore. With the limited review space, all four book reviews are always positive and the review for *Final Target* was no exception. I looked for a copy at my local library but they did not have it. When I was in a local bookstore, I bought a copy of the book, which is an oversized paperback. I've not started to read it yet but I would not have known about this book without reading the review. My local newspaper had significant influence for me.

Years ago I was the book review columnist for *Christian Parenting Today* (a magazine which no longer exists). I selected ten to fifteen books in a broad range of topics and genres for the audience, read the books and wrote my reviews. The magazine circulation was about 150,000 copies and I received stacks of "review copies" from various Christian and general market book publishers. In fact, it took continued maintenance to open the packages and see the various book possibilities—much less actually read and review the titles. My limited experience made me wonder how many books each week the book editor at the Arizona Republic receives for review consideration.

Here is a comparable example. In July 2009, Janice Harayda wrote a Soapbox column for *Publishers Weekly* called "Critics Don't Need Free Books." (www.snipr.com/freebk) For 11 years, Harayda worked as the book review editor for the *Plain Dealer* in Cleveland. Here's the sentence which stood out to me in her article: "At the *Plain Dealer*, I got **more than 400 books a week** from publishers, a landslide hard to handle even with another person helping me." The Sunday circulation of the *Plain Dealer* is similar to the Republic or 400,000.

See the long odds to get your book reviewed in a major city newspaper? These newspapers review about four books out of over 400 books that are received. Do you give up and not try to get book reviews? No, you simply try more niche-oriented markets where your probability is more likely for your book to be reviewed.

A recent *Publishers Weekly* article wrote about this topic of book reviews. Peter Hildick-Smith who works for Codex Group, a company which tracks the impact of reviews on sales said, "Reviews help both to raise awareness of a book and to persuade people to buy it."

Here's three websites which lists of places that review books: Karina Fabian has a length list of review sites (www.snipurl.com/kreview). The Complete Review contains 240 book review sites (www.snipr.com/compreview). Midwest Book Review has another great resource list of book review sites (www.snipr.com/otherreview).

As with any marketing effort for book reviews, consider several key elements. First, select your targeted publications carefully. Do they review your type of book? If so, how frequently do they publish reviews? Which editor handles the book reviews? Make sure you address the right person. Second, a key ingredient is follow-up. After a short period of time when you are certain the book has arrived, place a short phone call to simply see if the book has arrived and if it will be considered for review. Your conversation isn't chatty but short and professional. If the editor says they will be considering it, then call back in a few weeks and see if they had a chance to read the book. The follow-up shows you are expecting results from the review copy. Possibly your publisher is handling these book reviews.

The time and number of books that they encourage to be reviewed is limited. In a proactive way which encourages your partnership, ask your publisher's publicist for a list of publications where they are trying to get your book reviewed. Make it clear you want this list not to criticize their efforts but for you to go to the places where they <u>did not</u> promote your book.

Book reviews make a difference and are another element to include in your arsenal for marketing and promoting your book.

Offline Marketing Techniques

I've referred to a number of Internet based tools but don't neglect the efforts offline as well. For example, many authors have expanded their publishing careers and sold many books through the use of radio. Alex Carroll has been on more than 1,000 radio shows and sold over $1.5 million of books without a large promotion budget. You can learn about his techniques at: www.radiopublicity.com. Radio can be a valuable way to promote yourself and your publishing efforts.

A Never-Ending Supply

The marketing tools for promoting yourself and books continue to change. No one can predict the tool which you will be using next month or next year. My encouragement is to be aware and be willing to learn new tools. That next tool may be just the one you need to move into overdrive. You will not see these tools if you aren't aware of them and willing to experiment.

Recently I was listening to an interview with Raleigh Pinskey, author of *101 Ways to Promote Yourself.* I was fascinated to hear Pinskey explain her own shyness yet how she continually promoted this book with a 1999 copyright. Pinskey noted that her book continues to sell about 250 copies each month and had total sales at the time of over 10,000 copies. Now 250 copies a month may not sound huge to you but that translates into about 3,000 copies a year or a respectable number of copies.

As I heard this interview, something about the title, *101 Ways to Promote Yourself,* sounded familiar. The book had been on my shelf for at least six months or longer and I had never opened it. In the foreword, this book includes a classic marketing quote from P.T. Barnum, "Without promotion something terrible happens— nothing!" This quote captures the truth for many authors. They want the world to come to their door and when it does not, they don't understand. Like Pinskey explains, you can build the world's best mouse trap (or the world's greatest book) but if no one knows about it, then you have a garage (or basement or storage area), filled with great mouse traps (or books).

Make a choice as an author or writer to continually promote and market your book or yourself or both. It may not pay off immediately but in the long run, I predict you will reap unexpected and potentially huge results.

Dig Deeper

1. *Publicize Your Book!, An Insider's Guide to Getting Your Book the Attention It Deserves* by Jacqueline Deval (Perigee) 2008. Currently, the publisher at Hearst Books in New York, Jacqueline Deval has been a director of publicity for several publishing houses. She tells authors the inside scoop about how to effectively work with a publisher or on your own to generate publicity, be an asset to your publicist and get your book noticed. The book is loaded with invaluable information from someone who has paid her dues and worked on the inside of publishers. Catch her introduction, excerpts and endorsements at: www.publicizeyourbook.com

2. *Beyond the Bookstore, How to Sell More Books Profitably to Non-Bookstore Markets* by Brian Jud (Reed Business Press) 2004. Hardcover with CD-ROM. Have you ever read the sales numbers of a particular book and scratched your head wondering how that title sold in the bookstore? Some of those big sales numbers have sold outside of the bookstore. In fact, more than half of all books sold each year are sold outside of bookstores. Often an author believes their task is to write the best possible book, turn it over to the publisher and press on to the next project. It's always important to write the best possible book but more publishers are turning to the writer for sales assistance. This book is a valuable resource for any writer to think outside the box about how to sell their particular book. Jud covers 79 specific strategies for generating "special sales." These specific ideas can be incorporated into a nonfiction or fiction book proposal to show your publisher from the beginning that you will be proactive about special sales.

3. *How To Make Real Money Selling Books (Without Worrying About Returns), A Complete Guide to The Book Publishers' World of Special Sales* by Brian Jud, (Square One Publishers) 2009. This book helps you understand the non-trade market (outside the bookstore) and gives specific insider information about how to reach the non-trade non-retail markets such as businesses, associations, government agencies, the military marketplace and libraries. Or what about reaching the non-trade retail market like discount stores, airport bookstores, cable television shopping networks, museums, gift shops, specialty stores, book clubs and catalog marketing. Whether you want to reach some of these markets or any other type of book selling, this book is guaranteed to give you material to apply to your book marketing efforts with innovation from someone who has tackled these markets and educates you so you can become an insider. As Jud writes in the introduction, "The most important thing to remember is to look where everyone else has been looking, but see what no one else has seen. It sounds simple, and it is. But it is not easy. Persistence and determination are a must." (page 2) You will want to read this book several times and apply it to your marketing.

4. *Secrets of Social Media Marketing, How to Use Online Conversations and Customer Communities to Turbo-Charge Your Business!* By Paul Gillin (Quill Driver Books) 2009. At first glance, social media appears to be a huge waste of time yet repeatedly as I've experimented with the tools, I've found huge benefits and returns on my investment — often in surprising ways. Paul Gillin is an expert in this medium and you can learn a vast amount of insight from the pages of this book. And my resistance? It is rooted in my resistance to change. Gillin writes in the introduction, "Embracing change is the only sure success strategy in a business world that is evolving faster than we have

ever known. Students of the information technology industry know that failure to adapt to change can obliterate even larger and successful companies with blinding speed. In this book, I'll make the case that the changes now roiling the marketing world are the best thing that's ever happened to the profession. Start embracing these changes now and you'll propel your company and your career to new heights. Deny them, and you'll watch as the skills that have served you well for many years move rapidly toward irrelevance."

It's a small sample of what you will find inside this book. Throughout the book, various secrets are emphasized in simple words. He refers to many websites and tools to help you streamline and be effective with the various social media possibilities. Make full use of this book and return to it over and over. Read it with a highlighter with flags so you can spot the relevant places to apply for your own marketing efforts. Throughout this book, Gillin refers to numerous websites and tools. 5. *Grassroots Marketing for Authors and Publishers* by Shel Horowitz (AWM Books) 2007. This book contains a cornucopia of advice about the marketplace with practical ideas for creating a marketing plan and partnering strategies.

6. *The Frugal Promoter, How to Do What Your Publisher Won't* or *Nitty-Gritty How-Tos for Getting Nearly Free Publicity* by Carolyn Howard-Johnson (HowToDoItFrugally Publishing) 2011. This tremendous resource will also stir you to thinking about the marketplace and how to promote your printed work.

7. *Guerrilla Marketing For Writers, 100 Weapons to Help You Sell Your Work* by Jay Levinson, Rick Frishman, Michael Larsen, and David L. Hancock (Morgan James Publishing) 2010. The battle begins before your book even hits the shelves, and you need every

weapon to get ahead of the competition. *Guerrilla Marketing for Writers* puts and entire arsenal at your disposal. Packed with proven insights and advice, its details 100 "Classified Secrets" that will help to sell your work before and after it's published. Each "weapon" is rated by its monetary cost to the author, and well over half are free. The authors' overarching philosophy? Think like an entrepreneur.

8. *1001 Ways To Market Your Books, 6ᵗʰ Edition* by John Kremer (Open Horizons) 2006. Here are over 700 pages of proven marketing tips for authors so you can take an active role in marketing your books.

Awaken Your Dreams

1. This chapter covered a large array of tools to engage the market. Pick one tool and begin to explore it and learn about it. To jumpstart your publishing dreams, you need to be moving and actively looking for which tool will be the best for your situation. It will vary for different times in your life.

CHAPTER 20

Practice These Skills for a Lifetime

At the most inopportune time, this teacher shows up and demands my attention. The critical question is, when he arrives, will I see it as an opportunity or an obstacle? This teacher is adversity. No one that I know in publishing is immune to it, yet it continues to teach valuable lessons.

In a recent syndicated newspaper column, best-selling author Harvey Mackay wrote that adversity and perseverance are keys to success, saying,

> We must push through the adversity we face. If we don't, we will be poorly prepared for winning. People are successful because they face adversity head-on to gain strength and skill. They don't take the path of least resistance. Adversity is a powerful teacher....When you get discouraged, when you seem unable to make it, there is one thing you cannot do without. It is the priceless ingredient of success called

relentless effort. You must never give up. Success cannot be achieved without experiencing some adversity.[23]

Recently, I was about to launch a new audio product. I had prepared the audio files yet I could not get them into my shopping cart or figure out how to deliver them to the customer. I tried many different combinations without success and finally gave up at about 2 a.m. The next day, I asked advice from a friend who was much more knowledgeable about audio files. I learned that I was saving my audio files in the highest possible quality. There is a direct relationship between the size of the file and the quality of the audio. As the quality is higher, the file size will increase. I lessened the quality of the audio and the file became more manageable and something I could deliver to the customer. I was able to complete the project and once again my perseverance paid off.

Many people are amazed at the volume of my writing work. I didn't do it to amaze anyone. I'm convinced there are better writers and communicators in the marketplace who have published fewer books and written for fewer publications. But I do know I am doggedly persistent to work through the challenges of the day and discover the solutions.

If you haven't noticed, the publishing road is full of bumps, and you have to determine whether you will let those bumps become obstacles or opportunities.

Recently I ran into one. To launch the Ebook *Writing for the Christian Market* (www.writingchristianmarket.com), I offered a free teleseminar. For a portion of the teleseminar, I promoted the Ebook and announced that a mystery guest would join me on the call. This mystery guest was a magazine editor for one of the best places to break into the Christian magazine market who agreed to participate. I sent him details, then was extremely disappointed when he emailed back that he would not be able to participate because he would be teaching a weekly Bible study at exactly that same time period. It looked like my plans were ruined for my magazine editor mystery guest. Or was it?

I could have shrugged it and not had a guest editor—or I could use my extensive network from my years in this market and see if I could get another participant. I located an editor for a similar publication, called him, and he agreed to participate. This editor had never taught at a writer's conferences nor had he ever done a teleseminar, yet he was the main person who edited and selected the articles for his publication. Initially my situation looked like a challenge but it turned into something even better than my original plan.

I encourage you not to give up when something goes a different direction than you first planned. Look for a way to use the resources that you have, to make something even better happen. That persistence will pay off in the long run.

Choose a Different Path

I believe there are huge opportunities in publishing for everyone who chooses to be flexible. The publishing path is filled with obstacles and naysayers. Increasingly traditional publishers are closing their doors to unagented material. These doors are shut with good reason if they receive anything like the sample of material that arrived at my former agency.

If you could sit by the desk of an acquisitions editor or a literary agent, you would be shocked at the unprofessional pitches from well-intending authors. Like the recent nonfiction author who sent me a book proposal for a 150,000 word project. This author had a manuscript and had picked up my *Book Proposals That Sell* to learn how to create a book proposal. I applaud this author's commitment to learning about the business of publishing, yet he was overlooking something critical which would get his material continually rejected. It is highly unlikely that any traditional publisher will take a 150,000 word nonfiction book project. The normal upper limit of such a book is 70,000 to 80,000 words, and the author missed this critical detail to rejection-proof his submission. It's like the other lengthy novels that authors pitch to me without understanding the typical word length. Without knowing it, they are asking for rejection.

You must continue to learn everything you can about the business of publishing.

- How do book acquisitions editors and executives make decisions about which books to publish?

- What factors push them over the top about a particular book?

- How do book buyers make decisions about a particular book from a publisher?

Many of these factors shift and change and you need to be reading and learning about these elements so you can figure out how to stand apart from the typical editor pitch—in a positive way for that editor. As an acquisitions editor, besides looking for great writing, I'm always looking for that "X" factor. I'm talking about the little extras that the writer adds to the proposal or pitch which will rejection-proof the materials. The factors are different for each author but I've repeatedly mentioned some of the distinguishing factors. The biggest element is that publishers are looking for authors who understand the necessity of selling and promoting books. You'd be shocked at the resistance of some authors to work with the media or with their publisher to promote the book. The attractive authors are the ones who understand this factor and proactively work at it. Yes, I understand it's tiring but if you want to write books and stand apart, it's a necessity.

Beyond Expectations

When it comes to my writing, I work hard at it, turn it into the editor, work on rewrites (if needed), and then rejoice when it comes out in print. It could be a new book or a magazine article. I certainly have dreams and aspirations for my work. It's pretty dismal to learn that one of your books is going out of print. Or maybe you receive a quarterly or semi-annual or annual royalty statement and learn it's sold less than ten copies during that time period. Yes, it can happen and it has happened to me.

Some days I'm surprised with what has happened. Because of my body of work, each book was written with parameters. For example on some books, my name doesn't appear on the cover or title page, only on the copyright page. I wrote those books early on and in general as a work-made-for-hire, which means no additional earnings beyond the single paycheck. Some writers dislike this type of work but I've found it a productive way to make a living.

Recently I received an email about one of my early books, *Lighthouse Psalms*. Long out of print, I wrote those books over a brief period eight years ago. I wrote *Lighthouse Psalms* and *Love Psalms* which included short devotionals and verses from the Psalms. The only place my name appears is on the title page. I wrote them as work-made-for-hire, received a few author copies, and moved on to my next writing project. From discussions with the book packager and others, I knew those books sold at least 60,000 copies which are best-selling numbers. I hadn't thought about those beautiful books in some time. Then I received an email written in desperation from someone searching for a copy to help a dear friend to deal with an illness. She wrote, "This book has brought comfort to him over the last few months as I and other members of his family read to him from it. We then go to our Bibles and will look up the chapter in Psalms or particular passages and read the entire chapter. I cannot tell you the comfort that it brings to him when I read it." The email continued to explain that she couldn't locate the book but wanted to get a couple of copies. I don't have many copies of those books but I dug out what I had to send to this reader. I was stunned. Something that I wrote eight years ago continued to have an impact on someone's life. This response to my writing was definitely beyond any of my expectations.

Keep On Keeping On

If you watch the news or read the newspapers, it's easy to grow discouraged about the events of the world and your small sphere of influence over them. As you face different roadblocks in your writing, how do you handle them? Do you see those roadblocks as halting your progress or as one more thing that you have to overcome? Are these challenges obstacles, or opportunities? It's a matter of perspective.

I'm as human as the next person in this area but here's what I suggest when I face challenges to my writing life. Instead of wallowing in self-pity and discouragement (which is the easy route), I focus on what I can do to turn the situation around.

At Mega Book Marketing University, I heard the stories of Mark Victor Hansen and Jack Canfield as they were trying to find a publisher for the *Chicken Soup for the Soul* series. Today there are about 144 million copies of those books in print. Yet as Mark Victor Hansen mentioned in the foreword for this book, their proposal was rejected 140 times. In the face of such rejection, Jack and Mark learned to handle each rejection and say to each other, "Next." They had eliminated another publisher so what was next? Imagine what would have happened to them if they had given up with the 140th rejection?

These men had big dreams and goals for their writing and their words. When a small publisher in Florida, HCI Communications, published their books, they asked their publisher about his projections for the book. The publisher gave them a small expectation for sales and they instantly responded, "Well, that's not our goal."

The publisher asked them, "What's your goal?"

Mark said, "We want to sell a million and a half books in the first year." Their publisher laughed! Have you ever had anyone laugh at your goal? In the face of such laughter, Mark and Jack continued working and promoting their Chicken Soup books. It took 15 months until they met that goal and exceeded it.

I've got big dreams and plans for the future and some of them are wild but they will not happen if I keep the material stuck in my computer or in my desk drawer. It only happens as I'm out in the marketplace. I'd encourage you to keep on keeping on. Writing is a skill which plays into almost every field and discipline. You must set goals and pursue them in spite of any obstacle.

Dig Deeper

1. On Mark Victor Hansen's Web site, he includes a free MP3 download of the only gold record ever achieved for the spoken word: Earl Nightingale in *The Strangest Secret.* You can receive a copy of this recording at www.markvictorhansen.com or, if you prefer, you can watch the three-part You Tube video of at www.youtu.be/ajIRxdeCRZM.

Awaken Your Dreams

1. Download *The Strangest Secret* and either listen to it on your computer or watch the video. What practical steps can you take to implement the ideas in this presentation?

2. Plan now for discouragement and adversity to interfere with your publishing dreams. What steps are you taking to move through and beyond these situations and continue with your writing?

ABOUT THE AUTHOR

W. Terry Whalin is an acquisitions editor at Morgan James Publishing. For seven years, he was a book acquisitions editor at Howard Books, an imprint of Simon and Schuster and David C. Cook and he also ran his own literary agency for a couple of years. Terry's nonfiction writing has appeared in magazines like *Christianity Today, Writer's Digest, The Writer* and more than 50 other publications. Terry is an active member of The American Society of Journalists and Authors, which is the leading nonfiction writers group in the United States. He has written more than 60 nonfiction books including *Book Proposals That $ell: 21 Secrets To Speed Your Success.* To encourage writers of nonfiction and fiction, Terry is the creator of Right-Writing.com at: www.right-writing. com. Also his blog about the writing life at: www.thewritinglife.ws includes over 1,200 searchable entries. Terry and his wife, Christine, live in Colorado.

ENDNOTES

1   Dr. Seuss, *McElligot's Pool*, New York, NY, RandomHouse Books for Young Readers, 1947), p. 62, 64.

2   Susan Driscoll and Diane Gedymin, *Get Published!*, iUniverse, 2006, p. 5.

2   Ibid.

3   BookScan Web site: http://www.bookscan.com/controller.php?page=109

4   Publishing Poynters, Book and Information-Marketing News and Ideas from Dan Poynter, April 15, 2006, page 13-14.

5   Noah Lukeman, *The First Five Pages, A Writer's Guide to Staying Out of the Rejection Pile* (city, state: Fireside, 2000), p. 13.

6   Sheryl Fullerton and Naomi Lucks, *You Can Write!*, iUniverse, 2005, p. 171.

7   Dale Buss, *Family Man: The Biography of Dr. James Dobson* (city, state: Tyndale House, 2006), pp. 42-43.

8   *The First Five Pages*, pp. 195-97.

9   http://www.msnbc.msn.com/id/6953393/

10 http://www.forbes.com/lists/2006/53/T5P9.html

11 http://www.cesnur.org/2006/mi_brown_eng.htm

12 Lisa Rogak, *The Man Behind the Da Vinci Code* (city, state: Andrews McMeel Publishing, 2005), pp. 60-61.

13 http://www.nea.gov/news/news07/TRNR.html

14 Ali Pervez, *Marketing Is King* (city, state: Morgan James Publishing, LLC., 2007), pp. 222-23.

15 Dean R. Koontz, *How To Write Bestselling Fiction* (city, state:, Writer's Digest Books, 1981), p. 277.

16 Ibid, p. 278.

17 http://blog.bookmarket.com/2008/02/paulo-coelho-100-million-sales-and.html

18 Steven Van Yoder, *Get Slightly Famous* (city, state: publisher, copyright date), p. 3.

19 *Dan Poynter's Self-Publishing Manual*, Sixteen Edition/ Twentieth Printing 2007, Para Publishing, page 28.

20 Arielle Eckstut and David Henry Sterry, The Essential Guide to Getting Published (city, state: Workman, 2010), p. 105.

21 Ibid.

22 http://www.blogherald.com/2008/02/11/how-many-blogs-are-there-is-someone-still-counting/

23 http://timesunion.com/AspStories/storyprint.asp?StoryID=617013

INDEX

A

acquisitions editor, 18, 35, 43, 85, 164, 183, 191, 209, 216, 269-270

Allen, David, 38, 41

Amazon, 71, 159, 174, 193, 200, 236, 241, 248

Amazon Short, 71, 241

American Christian Fiction Writers, 143

American Society of Journalists and Authors, 107, 141, 144, 164, 166, 275

Andrews, Julie, 154

Association of Authors Representatives, 212

Author 101 University, 171

Authors Guild, 141-142, 186, 216

B

Barnes and Noble, 104, 156

bestseller, 45, 52, 62, 88, 104, 190, 200, 214, 227

Biagi, Shirley, 122

biographies, 52, 102, 103, 108, 224

blog, 149, 173, 176, 177, 242-245, 248-250, 253-255, 275

Blog Blaster, 255

blook, 242, 243

body of work, 54, 62, 147-149, 271

Book Proposals That Sell, 19, 149, 188, 193, 269

BookScan, 45, 46, 277,

Bowker, 36, 157

Brady, John, 122

Brown, Dan, 78-80

Buckingham, Jamie, 200, 202

Burby, Lisa, 233

C

Canfield, Jack, ii, 109, 237, 272

Carroll, Alex, 260

Carter, Jimmy, 137-138

Carter, Rosalynn, 137

Chandler, Stephanie, 159

Charisma, 114, 200

Chicken Soup for the Soul, i, ii, 29,237, 272

Christian Life, 129

Christian Parenting Today, 225, 258

Christianity Today, 48, 275

Coelho, Paulo, 151-152, 278

Colligan, Paul, 237

Colson, Chuck, 102

conference, writers, 19, 33, 35, 51, 58, 59, 60, 61, 73, 82, 101, 107, 137-139, 141, 143, 148, 152, 155-156, 162-168, 171, 174, 195, 197, 209, 225, 227, 238-239, 269

Cool, Lisa Collier, 93, 135

countdown timer, 39-41

craft, 18-19, 27-28, 33, 49, 51, 53, 57, 62-65, 72, 79-82, 99, 114-115, 119, 122-123, 140, 150, 152, 156, 159-160, 163, 165, 184, 189, 204, 225, 227, 231, 237

Crawford, Tad, 205

Creation House, 114

critique group, 47, 58, 66-67, 69-70,

Jumpstart Your Publishing Dreams
Order Form

Take The Next Step In Your Publishing Career:

_____ *Book Proposals That Sell Ebook*
www.bookproposals.ws $39.00

You can instantly get this best-selling Ebook which will show you step by step how to craft a book proposal.

_____ *Secrets About Proposals Teleseminar*
www.secretsaboutproposals.com $40.00

Eight top editors and literary agents from a diverse spectrum in publishing tell you what attracted them to a particular proposal. Immediately download this valuable teleseminar.

Also you can immediately download these two free Ebooks valued at over $84: *eBook Marketing Revealed, How to Write, Publish & Promote Your Own Profitable eBook!* and *Ghostwriters From the Inside Out.* Email terry@terrywhalin.com or register at our Web site: www.terrylinks.com/jump

Attention corporations, writing organizations, and writing conferences: Take 40 percent off and use our books as fundraisers, premiums, or gifts. Please contact the author.

CPSIA information can be obtained at www.ICGtesting.com
Printed in the USA
BVOW07*1144240914

368158BV00002B/2/P

9 781630 471125